WHAT'S IN YOUR BAG?

OUTCOME-BASED YOUTH MINISTRY

Developing Faith Skills in Young People

GARY AND LAURIE PECUCH

www.xulonpress.com

Table of Contents

Ephesians 2:8-10

For by grace you have been saved through faith,
and this is not your own doing; it is the gift of God –
not the result of works, so that no one may boast.
For we are what he has made us, created in Christ Jesus
for good works, which God prepared beforehand
to be our way of life. (NRSV)

*What about you? Are you ready for what God has in
store for you? Are you prepared? What faith skills are
you developing? What are you working on so you will be
equipped and ready when the Lord places and positions
you for His glory?*

The charge is not only to teach children and youth
about the faith, but also to provide opportunities for
them to be equipped in faith. In that way, they will
be ready for the good works which God has prepared
beforehand to be their way of life.

What's In Your Bag?

———————————

Two armies faced each other on opposite sides of a steep valley. On one side, the armies of Israel were encamped. On the other side, the Philistine army had gathered for war against Israel. A Philistine named Goliath, measuring over nine feet tall and wearing full armor came out each day for forty days taunting and challenging the Israelites to fight. His armor weighed 125 pounds. The tip of his spear was made of iron and weighed fifteen pounds. An armor bearer walked ahead of him carrying his shield. Truly, Goliath was a giant of a man.

One day, Goliath issued a challenge to the nation of Israel. "Choose one man to come out to fight me. If he kills me, then the Philistines will be your slaves. If I kill him, then you will be my slaves. Send out the best you have to fight me." Saul, the King of Israel, and the entire army of God were terrified and frozen in fear.

Meanwhile, David, the youngest son of Jesse, went back and forth several times from his home to the battle scene. He regularly visited his brothers to bring them food, but then needed to return quickly to help his father with their flock of sheep.

On one particular day, David was sent again to the battle lines by his father. While there, David heard Goliath shouting his daily taunt towards the armies of the living God. David responded, "Who is this uncircumcised Philistine that he should defy the armies of our God?"

Through faith and an eagerness to prove God would deliver, David volunteered to fight Goliath. King Saul's reaction to David's offer was less than enthusiastic. In fact, he thought David's offer was ridiculous. It made no sense to put the future of the entire nation of Israel on the shoulders of a young, untested teenager, especially if it meant fighting against a professional warrior like Goliath. But David persisted. He shared stories of protecting his father's sheep from lions and bears. Surely, if the Lord had rescued him from the claws of the lion and the bear, God would rescue him from a Philistine who had defied the armies of the living God!

It took some persuasion, but King Saul finally agreed to let David fight against the giant. Saul dressed David in his own armor, putting on David a bronze helmet, a coat of meshed metal, and then fastening his sword over David's tunic. David took several labored steps. "I can't wear this," David protested. "I am not used to them."

David took off Saul's armor and went to a nearby stream and selected five smooth stones. Dressed in his simple tunic, carrying his slingshot, and with five stones in his pouch, David started out across the valley and approached Goliath. The giant cursed at him, hurling threats and insults.

David soon found himself face-to-face with this giant of a man. The epic battle was about to begin. David was going to take on the greatest warrior the army of Israel had ever seen. It was just David (and the Lord God Almighty) against the best that evil could throw at him. Two entire armies were looking on. The stakes were high. It was winner take all.

Confident in his faith, David stepped forward, telling Goliath, "You come to me with a sword, a spear, and a javelin, but I come to you in the name of the Lord of hosts, the one true God of Israel; this battle is the Lord's, and He will deliver you into my hand."

> **In essence, David had been preparing for this moment all of his life. He had in his bag what he knew how to use... a skill he had developed over time.**

As Goliath moved in for the kill, everything David had become up to this point in his life came into play. David was a young man devoted to God and family. He was a teenager who had learned over time the skill of using a stone and sling. He had spent hours practicing hitting targets. He had battled vicious predators and won. He had an uncompromising faith. In essence, David had been preparing for this moment all of his life. He had in his bag what he knew how to use...a skill he had developed over time. God brought him to this place, at this moment in time, because David had both the faith and the skill necessary to take on the giant.

David reached into his bag and pulled out one small smooth stone. He placed it in his sling. As Goliath moved forward, David swung the sling over his head. He released the stone. It hit Goliath and he fell hard to the ground. The army of Israel stood momentarily in disbelief. Then, realizing what had just happened, they erupted into shouts of victory and praise. All of David's preparation had paid off. God had taken David's skill and used it for His glory.

What about you? Are you ready for what God has in store for you? Are you prepared? Can you, like David, reach into your bag and pull out what you need to successfully get the job done? What skills are you developing? What are you working on so you will be prepared when the Lord places and positions you for His glory?

Our charge is not only to teach children and youth about the faith, but to provide opportunities for them to be equipped with what we call "Faith Stones." Faith Stones are skills that will enable young people to develop a meaningful relationship with their Creator, themselves, and others. Faith Stones are skills they develop, have in their Faith Bag, and are readily on-hand to be pulled out when needed. Faith Stones are skills that can be used by God to touch the lives of others.

What skills are in your bag? What skills are you helping to put into the bags of the young people in your life?

Like David, we need to be ready for what God has for us. We need to be prepared!

Corey: Our Modern Day David

When Corey was in fifth grade, I asked, "Corey, what would you like to do when you grow up?"

Without hesitation, she eagerly replied, "I want to be a Camp Counselor at Camp Luther!"

Knowing Corey's family history, I was not surprised by her answer. Corey's family had been attending a week of family camp long before Corey was born. Her grandparents went to Camp Luther. Her parents went to Luther. Aunts, uncles, and cousins joined them on this family vacation. Corey, as long as she could remember, had gone there every summer and had loved every moment of the week–the camp songs, the camp skits, the talent shows, swimming, the campfires, walks in the woods, the traditional camp foods and desserts (especially s'mores), and the creative programming. Then there were the camp counselors…about 20 college age students who made the week at camp fun, memorable, and a rewarding experience. They were good role models for young people like Corey.

So I said to Corey, "Well, Corey, we have seven years until you will be old enough to be a camp counselor. It's my job (as your congregational youth director) to partner with your parents to help prepare you for where God is leading you in life. Let's start by making a list of what you need to be able to do to be the best camp counselor Camp Luther has ever seen."

Corey's eyes lit up. She immediately became engaged in the process. I knew the next time I saw Corey she would have a list for me.

Sure enough, she did! Corey had developed a list of skills that every camp counselor needed to have in her bag. The list included activities such as leading songs, giving devotions, giving a campfire talk, leading games, leading mixers, creating and performing skits, starting campfires, being a good role model, leading Bible Studies, and, of course, making s'mores.

Essentially, Corey had written a sketch of a personal ministry plan. A plan, created by her, to help her get ready for what she felt the Lord was leading her to do. Typically, I ask students to prayerfully consider their interests, their gifts, their experiences, and to prayerfully think through their personal ministry plans. Often personal ministry plans take time to mature into a clear sense of direction and purpose. Corey's plan had been developing for years as she attended Camp Luther. That's all we needed. We got to work!

After connecting and involving her parents, our congregation gave Corey regular opportunities to be taught, trained, and to practice the various key elements of being a good camp counselor. She learned how to plan and lead devotions for children. She was trained and given the opportunity to lead songs at our weekly elementary school age club. She became an expert at developing faith-based skits. It was impressive to watch her take a theme or Bible passage and create a quality skit, often in ten minutes. By the time she was a junior in high school, Corey was working with younger children to develop a weekly skit for the club opening. She attended our Intentional Relationship Building Skills training (Faith Stone 8) and Faith-Based Story Talk Skills training (Faith Stone 21) multiple times to learn how to initiate conversations and speak in front of groups. We touched on every aspect of her camp counselor personal ministry plan. By the time she applied for a position at Camp Luther, Corey was prepared. Her bag was full. She was ready.

At the time of this writing, Corey has completed her second summer as a camp counselor. Yep, at Camp Luther! Corey is living out her dream. She loves it, the camp loves her, and she plans to go back next summer. And, oh yeah, hundreds of campers have had their faith touched, enhanced, and deepened by Corey's efforts. *To God be the Glory!*

AND, as a result of this experience with Corey, the concept of Outcome-Based Youth Ministry was born.

Outcome-Based Youth Ministry

Outcome-Based Youth Ministry is now one of our core philosophies of ministry. It is a list of assets and skills we intentionally build into young people throughout their school years. As we saw with Corey, the concept necessitates having an end goal in mind and prayerfully developing and creating a road map to meet that desired result. The intention is to partner with parents and together encourage and equip young people to develop a plan for personal growth. This personal growth plan is a tool to define the necessary assets needed to love God, gain self-awareness, serve others, and glorify Him.

Outcome-Based Youth Ministry fulfills the biblical mandate of church leaders found in Ephesians 4:12-13...

Their responsibility is to equip God's people to do his work and build up the church, the body of Christ. This will continue until we all come to such unity in our faith and knowledge of God's son that we will be mature in the Lord, measuring up to the full and complete standard of Christ. (NLT)

The goal then is to help youth prepare for ministry by doing what David did. That is, to help them "pick up" stones to place in their bags so that when ministry moments arise, they are prepared to meet the ministry need. I want youth to be able to confidently reach into their bags and pull out a needed Faith Stone. This preparation can be anything from stepping forward to say a table grace at mealtime (Faith Stone 28) to making good decisions based on their personal written standards (Faith Stone 11) to stepping up to facilitate a Bible study for a group of friends (Faith Stone 25).

In Outcome-Based Youth Ministry, we ask parents, "What aspects of faith do you want your child to develop?" As a congregation, we ask ourselves, "What Faith Stones do our young people need in order to be prepared for a life of service and devotion to our Lord and Savior Jesus Christ?" Ultimately, we want to offer children and youth the opportunity to develop as many Faith Stones as possible so their bags will be overflowing in preparation for the various scenarios they will encounter throughout life.

The role of the congregation in the life of a young person is to point him/her toward Christ and help him/her to develop a relationship with Him. Then, as we partner with parents, we train and equip our children with necessary skills so that they may live out their devotion to Christ. In essence, we help them fill their Faith Bags with Faith Stones for deepening their personal faith, while at the same time preparing them to touch the lives of others.

Faith Stones will aid young people in self-discovery, incorporate spiritual disciplines into their lives, and equip children and youth with ministry skills to live out their personal leading in life. As a young person grows in faith and begins to develop a personal mission or direction in life, the Faith Stones on which we work can become more specific in nature.

As I travel around to congregations, I am often asked, "How do we keep our kids coming to church?" While that is a worthwhile question, our most important goal is to provide a faith foundation that will equip our children and youth for life. It is time for congregations to develop a long-term, results-oriented strategy for children, youth, and family ministry. We need a vision that equips our youth with a faith and the necessary skills that prepare them for life. The sooner we implement faith skills, the better. We can start with high school youth, but our experience has shown us that developing faith skills in elementary and middle school youth is a better place to start. We then visit and revisit the concepts throughout a youth's middle school and high school years. Aiding youth in their faith maturity and helping them to develop Faith Stones will prepare them to be used by the Lord in whatever position or situation they are placed throughout their lives. Like David, we want our high school graduates to be fully confident and prepared with a bag full of Faith Stones so they can give God the glory as they take on giants in life.

> For updated information on
> Outcome-Based Youth Ministry visit
> www.faithwebbing.com

Consider Culture

In 2003, St. John's Lutheran Church in Grove City, Ohio, where I serve as Youth Ministry Coordinator, was honored to be asked to participate in a national study sponsored by the Lily Foundation called the Exemplary Youth Ministry Study (www.exemplarym.com). The study was the largest ever conducted on the topic of congregational youth ministry. The intent was to identify and survey individuals associated with successful youth ministries. The survey covered an equal number of small, medium, and large congregations. Seven denominations and 131 congregations were involved in the study: Assemblies of God, Evangelical Covenant, Evangelical Lutheran Church of America, The Presbyterian Church (USA), Roman Catholic, Southern Baptist, and The United Methodist Church. The goal was to survey and dialogue with congregations that were having a meaningful and sustained positive impact on developing faith in teenagers. St. John's was asked to participate by surveying 30 teens, 30 non-parental adults, and 30 parents. The survey was extensively made up of multiple choice questions and took over an hour to complete. Once the results were available, my wife and I attended a two day presentation of the results of the study led by researcher Dr. Roland Martinson of Luther Seminary (St. Paul, Minnesota).

The study revealed much and its website is worth visiting. The two day presentation initially revealed to me that successful youth ministry programs create a healthy "culture" specific to their congregation. Although not a rocket science of a discovery, it helped to confirm what we had already stumbled upon within our congregation. That is, the importance of purposefully creating a healthy children's, youth, and family ministry culture within the congregation. Left to chance, the culture of a church community can often quickly disintegrate. All one has to do is look out our church windows, and we see a world full of distractions that can pull youth away from their faith-filled purpose.

The Exemplary Youth Ministry study results confirmed that successful congregational ministries have created their own unique healthy cultures. Each congregational culture has its own uniquely shared vision, goals, standards, activities, holiday traditions, worship services, food rituals, special music, annual summer excursions, and impact events. These shared values and experiences define a church's culture. Most of these successful congregational customs have intentionally been developed over time. In an ever-changing world, youth benefit from identifying well established routines, traditions, and rituals within their congregation and its youth ministries.

With this in mind, consider how you would go about creating or enhancing your own culture of being an equipping church. What do you envision for your youth? What faith practices would you implement to reach that end result?

At our church, we have decided to build our culture around three foundational philosophies as we strive to be salt and light in the world for our loving Savior:

1. Building a loving, caring, intergenerational community based on affirmation and support through Faith Webbing;
2. Outcome-Based Ministry, where our goal is to help young people develop their faith skills; and

3. Service to Others, where we give youth specific opportunities and responsibilities to use their developing skills in service to Christ.

We are determined to love "the stuffing" out of our children and youth while building into them the necessary Faith Stones needed to live out their personal calling in life.

Take It Slowly, but Start Now

It is worth mentioning that creating a new culture in a congregation takes time. More often than not, creating a healthy culture for youth takes a bit of change in either philosophy or types of programming. The very thought of "change" itself can cause angst among church-goers. Don't rush it. We need to intentionally take the necessary time to define who we want to become, what standards we are going to live by, and then develop a plan to ease the implementation of the culture changes within the ministry.

The purpose of this book is to introduce the concept of Outcome-Based Youth Ministry, to share the list of Faith Stones that we are building into our young people, and then to offer some ideas on how you can develop Faith Stones in the lives of your youth. The hope is that you will catch a glimpse of the concept and then begin to envision how Outcome-Based Youth Ministry and building Faith Stones in young people might best fit into your congregational or educational setting.

Our Faith Stone list is constantly evolving. It changes with the needs of the students, our ministry goals, and, most importantly, where God is leading our students. Keep in mind that each young person, each church, and each situation is beautifully unique. The Faith Stones you develop and implement with your students (or your child) will likely look different. Thus, the intent of this book is not to get you to implement the list of Faith Stones that we have developed, but to encourage you to think through what skills need to be in the Faith Bags of those you are charged with nurturing.

As you read through these pages, prayerfully think through what assets your young people need to develop. Start a list of skills and ideas that will prepare your youth for a life of devotion to Christ. Bring others on board with the concept of Outcome-Based Youth Ministry. Then begin to work through a plan for implementing your ideas.

My advice is to read through this book thinking about which Faith Stones would be best or easiest to introduce to your church environment. I would start with simple enhancements like teaching children and youth how to say table grace (Faith Stone 28), introduce Thankful Lists (Faith Stone 14), or start young people praying through their purpose on a regular basis (Faith Stone 1). Once identified, these key result areas become the outcomes that you are hoping to achieve. By doing so, you have taken the first steps to designing an outcome-based ministry. As some ideas will work well in your setting, you may find that others may not. Do not get discouraged. There are many Faith Stones worth considering. In our congregation we introduce two or three new enhancements to the ministry each year. We all know how times flies. It will not be long before you will be able to look back and see several positive, healthy new directions that will benefit not only youth, but possibly your entire congregation.

Keep in mind there is no particular order to the faith stones listed in this book. We have numbered the faith stones simply for the purpose of easy reference.

So here we go! May the good Lord bless you as we journey together in preparing young people to love and serve our Lord.

> For a jump start visit contact Gary through
> www.faithwebbing.com

WAIT! The Most Important Part...

W e can't begin to talk about the specific Faith Stones until we talk about the purpose of it all. David reached into his bag to pull forth stones to defeat Goliath. The bag was the perfect place for David to carry his carefully chosen five smooth stones. It was always with him as he defended the sheep and traveled to bring food to his brothers. The bag held stones David needed for what God had in store for him. The bag was the place to hold what he needed to show God's glory.

Imagine, for us, the bag is the Gospel. The Gospel surrounds all that we are and all that we do. Hearing and taking to heart the good news of Christ's death and resurrection gives us eternal hope. Our life takes on new significance as we dearly hold the Gospel near to us. As believers, everything we do is about the Good News of Jesus Christ. Without Christ, it is all worthless. With Christ, everything has meaning. Without Christ, the list of Faith Stones is but a mere list of attributes to be acquired so one can get ahead in life. With Christ, the Faith Stone list becomes a treasure of skills that when implemented will have eternal significance.

Youth of all ages need to understand the basics of the Good News. Basics, once understood, will be the foundation for faith formation, values, goal setting, and decision making. Once children and youth grasp who they are and *whose* they are, they will have direction, purpose, and a reason for wanting to develop the Faith Stones they need.

There are various ways to share the Good News of Jesus Christ to young people. As we worked with the youth at our church, we needed to come up with a way to explain the Gospel so that it was easy for the youngest of believers to understand, yet still viable for adolescents in high school. It needed to be an explanation of the Gospel in the context of the reality of the world in which we live.

Thus, we use this simple five point message of the Good News as we tell the story. We often draw pictures on the dry erase board helping youth to visualize the points.

1. In the beginning, God created a wonderful world, and at the end of every creation day, God looked at what was created and said, "It is good." *(Genesis 1:4, 1:10, 1:12, 1:18, 1:21, 1:25, 1:31)* Life on earth was good. Adam and Eve's relationship with God was also good.

2. Sin entered the world and along with it came evil, pain, and suffering. Mankind's relationship with the Creator was severed. The world was no longer good but broken with sin. Because of this, we live in a broken world and we experience its brokenness. *(Romans 3:23, Romans 5:12-14)*

3. God sent his Son, Jesus, to die on the cross for our sins and to rise again conquering death and evil. Jesus bridges the gap so that we can be redeemed and returned to a right relationship with our Creator. We need to embrace what Christ has done for us on the cross. God loves us so very much. *(John 3:16 & Romans 6:23)*

4. At the end of our lives, God promises believers that we will be in His presence forever. We have a heavenly hope. God's promise offers us hope and strength to live in this broken world. *(Philippians 3:20 & I Peter 1:4)*

5. With the time we have between this life and the next, we strive to grow in faith and love by living a godly life, becoming a "polished arrow", and being available to be used by God to help piece this broken world back together. *(Isaiah 49:1-3 & James 1:27)*

Wow! How profoundly simple! Even first graders can understand this concept. Children respond eagerly when they know and believe God loves them, wants to be in relationship with them, and with the help of the Holy Spirit, wants to work through them to share the love of Christ with others. God is the Great Redeemer. In a broken world, through Christ, we become His hands and feet offering redemptive acts of grace and mercy. Love is the glue which helps piece a broken world together until Christ's return.

Thus, the main purpose of our lives is to develop a relationship with our Creator and then to allow Jesus to work through us to touch the lives of others. Children and youth get excited about the fact that the God of the universe has chosen them to be His hands and feet to touch lives and make an eternal impact on others. Once children and youth understand this simple concept, they are quick to volunteer for activities and projects which will allow others to experience Jesus for themselves.

We explain this simple concept to children beginning in elementary school and revisit the lesson over and over again as they move through their teen years. The benefits of young people understanding this simple concept is that children and youth...

- hear the message of the Gospel in a way they can understand
- learn there is life after physical death
- have an understanding of their role here on earth
- eagerly respond to God's call for them to help mend this broken world
- see themselves as an asset and part of the solution to the world's problems
- redirect their focus off of themselves as they become more compassionate in caring for those who are suffering
- understand they are an important part of the church of today
- appreciate how they can immediately make a positive eternal impact on the lives of others
- realize they have a God-given purpose
- have hope for today, along with a hope for a heavenly future

In our society and especially within the church, children and youth are often sent the message that they are a liability. They are too loud. They should not be running around the building. They break things. They wear inappropriate attire. They have too many body piercings. They have unusual hair styles. They are constantly playing with their cell phones. They are lazy, have no commitment, no loyalty or drive. The message they hear is they are going to have to change in order to fit in here, which translates to them that they are not accepted and loved by God until they make some changes in their lives.

Granted, some of the above may be true, but we **choose** to see youth with our "Jesus glasses." We know Jesus loves each young person and sees each one's heart, a heart created to love and be loved by God. As a church, we need to send the message to young people that they are worthy, loveable, and have a purpose and mission in life. We believe that they do! When young people feel like they are an asset to the kingdom of God, they flourish and develop a biblical self-esteem.

Truly understanding the message of the Good News gives young people the opportunity to feel good about their faith, the church and its mission, and their role in the Kingdom of God. And that's way worth it.

Here are some typical comments I hear from youth in our congregation.

"Gary, is there room for me to go to Faith Mission?"

"Will there be enough room for me to be a cabin coach this summer at Adventure Camp?"

"Gary, are there any more bicycles to assemble?"

"When does the Bed Brigade meet again?"

"Where are we going on our service trip this summer?"

"When are we going shopping for the Grove City food pantry?"

"Gary, when are we going Christmas caroling to our homebound members?"

Each service project sign-up sheet in our congregation has a healthy number of youth names on it. Many have a waiting list. As students gain a good understanding of the gospel and how they can be a part of the redemptive work of Jesus Christ, it prompts them into service.

When Libby was in fourth grade, she saw a girl on TV who had collected shoes for an orphanage in Africa. Libby, understanding the basic message of the Good News and understanding God wants to work through her to touch the lives of others, approached us with an idea to collect shoes to send to children who had no shoes. So, with some coaching from her parents and us (her congregational youth directors), Libby ventured out on her mission. She linked up with a mission group in our congregation who annually spends a week in Baja California (Mexico) with children from a local orphanage. She came up with a plan. She began advertising in our church that she was collecting shoes for children in Mexico. Libby also decided that instead of friends and family giving her birthday gifts on her birthday, she wanted them to donate shoes for this new ministry she was developing. She set up stations around the church and even advertised her mission idea in her classroom at school. Soon Libby started gathering pairs of shoes from family, friends, schoolmates, and church folks. In less than two months, Libby collected over 300 pairs of shoes. Some came as far away as Alabama. At her birthday party, which took place at the picnic shelter behind the church, there was a celebration with Libby and her shoes. Soon after her birthday, the shoes were sent to Mexico.

Libby knows Jesus. She understands her purpose in life is to develop a loving relationship with God. Libby also knows that she is the hands of Jesus, allowing herself to be used to help piece a broken world back together. Libby's way of putting a broken world back together was to provide shoes for children. Libby has a faith. She understands how God can use her in the lives of others, and Libby is a minister of the Gospel. How great is that!

THE FAITH STONES

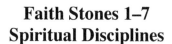

Faith Stones 1–7
Spiritual Disciplines

The first seven Faith Stones are organized into a category of Spiritual Disciplines.

Spiritual Disciplines are the foundation of our daily walk with Jesus. These disciplines are essential to an active and growing faith. With them, we grow strong and true. Once established, these routines can be part of a lifetime faith walk of growth and service.

"Early and often" is the cry as we begin to introduce these disciplines to youth. We place an emphasis on having the disciplines introduced, understood, and hopefully on their way to being established in youth by the time they complete middle school. Fifth through seventh grade students tend to be eager to learn and generally wish to take on responsibilities. We hope by the time students reach high school, we have woven spiritual disciplines into their lives; disciplines that will carry them into adulthood.

Faith Stone 1

Live Your Purpose in Life

I know several men who served our country as Marines. One of them is a good friend of mine. Through personal discussions and hearing Marines speak through media outlets, I have always been impressed by the clear sense of direction, purpose, and mission that each Marine possesses. Asking my friend about the topic, he simply said, "In the Marines, you did not have to figure out what your purpose was. It was told to you, 'Defending our nation at home. Protecting her interests abroad.'" Every Marine is united in mind and intent on that purpose. The statement is simple, easy to remember, practical, and effective.

For the faith-based person, his or her purpose comes from the Lord God Almighty. There are several scripture verses or passages that can be used to define our purpose in life. We have chosen to use the written words of Moses, spoken again to us by Christ.

You shall love the Lord your God with all your heart, and with all your soul, and with all your strength. (Deuteronomy 6:5, NLT)

The statement is simple, easy to remember, practical, and effective. It is a direct command from the Lord God Himself, given to us through Moses. It is a well-worded purpose. It is also wonderfully simple. I sometimes think of the multitudes of people throughout history who have spent their entire lives searching for purpose and meaning. What a comforting advantage it is to accept the God-given purpose told to us through Moses.

Because I work with children and youth in a congregational setting, I need to explain the Christian faith in simple terms. These terms need to be simple enough that even an elementary age child can understand.

I hand students their life's purpose directly from the word of God. They are instructed to write Deuteronomy 6:5 on several 3 x 5 inch index cards and then place the cards in conspicuous places that are a part of their normal morning routine (night stand, bathroom mirror, in their Bible). We ask, instruct, and tell youth to prayerfully read this verse every day before they leave the house.

Students are encouraged to personalize the verse and write a prayer on their 3 x 5 card that looks like this...

Lord, help me today to love you with all my heart, and with all my soul, and with all my strength. Amen.

Imagine how one's mind can become transformed by simply praying one's purpose every day. This verse eventually becomes memorized and brought back to mind throughout the day by the Holy Spirit. It becomes a constant reminder of what we are to be doing at every turn in the ups and downs of daily living.

I believe looking into your Faith Bag and seeing a known purpose for your life, given to you by Almighty God, has to be one of the greatest treasures one can possess.

My purpose:

You (I) shall love the Lord your (my) God with all your (my) heart, and with all your (my) soul, and with all your (my) strength.

- Deuteronomy 6:5

Faith Stone 2

Live Your Job Description

There is a great story near the end of the second chapter of Luke. It's the story where Jesus and his family go to Jerusalem for the Passover festival. When the festival is over, Joseph and Mary leave Jerusalem with an entire caravan of people. And, after a full day of travel, they are unable to locate Jesus. Frantic, they head back to Jerusalem. According to Luke, it took a three day search for Jesus' parents to find him. You know the story; they finally find him in the synagogue talking to church leaders. The chapter powerfully ends with verse 52. It says, "Jesus grew in wisdom and stature and in divine and human favor."

What a great verse! A few years ago, while preparing to teach this passage to middle school students, it dawned on me that Luke 2:52 is a great four point outline for a daily job description.

Similar to what we do in our congregation for knowing our purpose, I instruct youth to write Luke 2:52 on several 3 x 5 inch index cards. I ask them to word it this way...

My job today is to grow physically, grow spiritually, to earn the respect of others, and to please God.

Like the purpose verse, how wonderfully simple and easy it is to understand. Even an elementary school age child can grasp the concept. Then, as youth grow and mature, Luke 2:52 can take on deeper meaning, lead to deeper discussions, and can be used for self-evaluation each day.

The technique can also be used by a family or group to talk through their recent experiences. Whenever we are away from home, our church group uses the four elements in Luke 2:52 to begin the process of evaluating our day. The concept has worked well in a variety of settings.

This is how we explain the four parts of Luke 2:52:

1. **We are to grow physically** (in stature) by taking care of our bodies, by eating well, and having some type of physical activity each day. It seems not a week goes by that I do not read a newspaper headline, a magazine article, or hear a sound bite on radio or television about the importance of eating well and regularly exercising. Even my healthcare provider rewards my exercise efforts with dollars I can put towards healthcare costs.

2. **We are to grow spiritually** (in wisdom) by growing in maturity, developing faith qualities that are listed in the bible, such as Galatians 5 and II Peter 1.

   But the fruit of the Spirit is love, joy, peace, forbearance, kindness, goodness, faithfulness, gentleness and self-control. Against such things there is no law. (Galatians 5:22 & 23, NIV)

   For this very reason, make every effort to add to your faith goodness; and to goodness, knowledge; and to knowledge, self-control; and to self-control, perseverance; and to perseverance, godliness; and to godliness, mutual affection; and to mutual affection, love. For if you possess these qualities in increasing measure, they will keep you from being ineffective and unproductive in your knowledge of our Lord Jesus Christ. (II Peter 1:5-8, NIV)

3. **We are to earn the respect of others** (in human favor) by being people of honesty, integrity, and responsibility. In my daily dealings with people, I want my actions to be above reproach. When introducing this idea, I make the point that earning the respect of others does not mean we are to live our lives to please others. There are plenty of people in my life whom I disagree with on various issues but whom I greatly respect. Likewise, I know people who disagree with me on certain topics, yet I have earned their respect.

4. And finally, **we are to live a life pleasing to God** (in divine favor). With younger children, we tell them what a godly life looks like. We talk about the Ten Commandments, what is right and wrong, and how we should treat others. With older students, we explore scripture together, looking up verses on holiness such as Leviticus 19:2 *(be holy for I am holy)*, Philippians 1:27 *(conduct yourself in a manner worthy of the Gospel)* and those great passages Paul wrote about living a life pleasing to God as seen in I Thessalonians 4. We pray these passages speak into the depths of students' hearts and that they hear the Holy Spirit's call for holy living.

Process Each Day

What I encourage young people to do each day is to combine their purpose and job description verses into a spiritual discipline. I recommend they start each day by praying through their life's purpose, and then, at the end of their day, either with another person or before they fall asleep, process their day with the job description verse. It is good for them to ask themselves, "How did I do today physically? Did I eat well? Did I have any physical activity?"

"How did I grow today spiritually? Am I closer to my Creator this evening than when I woke up this morning? Was I sensitive to the leading of God's spirit? Where did I see God today?"

"How did I do in earning the respect of others? Did I do well today in my relationships? Is there a relationship in my life that needs some attention? Is there someone I need to forgive or from whom I should ask forgiveness?"

Then finally, it is good for them to ask themselves, "Did I live a life pleasing to God today? If so, what did I do? If not, how can I do better tomorrow?"

So, the day is *started* by being reminded of one's life purpose (Faith Stone 1). The day is *invested* living out the four point job description (Faith Stone 2). And then the day is *ended* processing the results. It is simple, straight forward, and even the youngest believer can do it. If young people simply develop and nurture this spiritual discipline, they will find themselves walking side-by-side with the Lord their entire lives.

Knowing your purpose in life and having an easy to remember spiritual format for processing your day are two Faith Stones worth having in your Faith Bag.

Faith Stone 3

Develop a
Meaningful Prayer Life

———————⁓———————

Prayer is such a vast subject. There are a gazillion ways to pray. What we hope to do is to give teens a tool and a format that will help make it easier for them to develop a spiritual discipline of having a meaningful prayer life.

One of the ways we do this is by helping youth to develop a prayer notebook. In this notebook, we place items that will give teens topics to pray through. For some students they have a notebook just for prayer. For other students, prayer becomes a section in their Visionary Notebook. I will talk more about the Visionary Notebook later. For now, let's take a look at how a student can prayerfully use a notebook to develop the Prayer Faith Stone.

First, we give each student what we call the "Everyday Prayer Sheet." This sheet is a tool students can use to pray through items that are important to them. At the top of the sheet are a few things we think would be good for them to pray through daily. Students then get to personalize the sheet by adding things to pray for that are of importance to them. The sheet tends to be the first page in their prayer notebook.

Second, we give students a prayer format that they can use during times of prayer. This format offers a progression of prayer that will help them to stay focused. In this progression of prayer, students start by centering first on God, and then on others, and then on themselves. Here is the four stage format.

1. Pray through your Thankful List
2. Pray through Confession
3. Pray for Others
4. Pray for Yourself

Praying through your Thankful List

We encourage young people to begin a prayer time with thanksgiving by praying through several items on their thankful list. The concept of the thankful list is Faith Stone 14: Grow Thankfulness. We want youth to start by spending a few minutes reflecting on all that they have been given and thanking God for their many blessings.

When using this prayer format, students begin by praying with their focus on God, His character, and thanking Him for being the giver of all good gifts. They then direct their focus on confession.

Praying through Confession

The next part of the prayer session is confession. For this time, we ask young people to bring lists they have previously created called Know Your Standards (Faith Stone 11) and Find Your Million Dollar Mate (Faith Stone 22).

The first list contains written standards to live by that each student personally created. As students pray through their standards, they are asking God to help them to live lives pleasing to Him, while at the same time they get a chance to confess shortcomings of not living up to their personal standards.

The second list contains previously determined qualities they are looking for in a potential spouse. As an example, a young person may have listed that he or she wants a future spouse who is honest. So we ask each student to rank him or herself in the area of honesty on a scale from one to five. Valuing honesty, the student reflects on how he or she is doing. The emphasis is placed on not just finding the right spouse but becoming the right spouse.

During the confession time, we want students to reevaluate how they are doing with their standards and being a person of character. Have they met their standard? Where have they not lived up to being a person of integrity? What qualities do they need to work on?

We explain to youth that as they do this process, they may realize they have not met their standard of being completely honest, for example, so they can pray a prayer of confession that goes something like this...

Lord, I have not been fully honest in all of my relationships. I ask for your forgiveness. Please bring to mind anyone that you think I should ask for his or her forgiveness. Help me as I strive to be a more honest person. Amen.

We hope youth will read through their lists and recognize and confess any sin the Holy Spirit draws to their attention. As they effectively face sin, they can walk in grace and strive to live a life worthy of the Gospel.

Now that students have spent prayer time focusing on God through thanksgiving and confession, they can move into praying for others.

Praying for Others

The word of God tells us to take time to pray for others.

*I urge, then, first of all, that petitions, prayers, interces-
sion and thanksgiving be made for all people.* (I Timothy
2:1, NIV)

*And pray in the Spirit on all occasions with all kinds of
prayers and requests. With this in mind, be alert and always
keep on praying for all the Lord's people.* (Ephesians
6:18, NIV)

Thus, we also encourage students to pray for others. We
do this by having youth dedicate a section of their notebook
to friends and family. We have a day when we ask students
to bring pictures of important people in their lives to a youth
group meeting. With construction paper, glue, tape, and
markers, students then create a page or collage of family and
friends. Once completed, students place their prayer pages in
protective sheets and put the pages in their prayer notebook
or their visionary notebook.

During the students' prayer time, they can then turn to a
page dedicated to their father, place their hand on the page,
and pray for their dad. Next, they turn the page and put their
hand on a picture of their mom and pray silently for mom.
Students often have pages dedicated to siblings, friends, and
even pets. They turn the pages one by one, pausing to pray
for each important person in their lives. Some youth even
create a church page with pictures of the building, pastors,
and ministries of the church.

Praying For Yourself

Now that the youth have had a time of thanksgiving, confession, and praying for others, they can now pray for themselves. These are personal prayers of hopes, dreams, fears,
relationships, concerns, etc. Many youth refer back to their
everyday prayer sheet for this portion of their prayer time.

As mentioned at the outset of this chapter, prayer is a vast subject. What we have done here is to share one prayer format we give youth in order to help them to incorporate some sort of prayer routine into their lives: a workable format they can return to time and time again. The format we discussed here has worked well for us and is another Faith Stone youth can place in their Faith Bag.

An example of an "Everyday Prayer Sheet" can be found in the appendix

Faith Stone 4

Develop Bible Study Habits

W e believe it is important for every believer to be in
a regular (weekly or biweekly) faith growth group
throughout their entire life. In Acts we read about the early
church and its faith practice.

*They worshiped together at the temple each day, met in
homes for the Lord's Supper, and shared their meals with
great joy and generosity all the while praising God and
enjoying the goodwill of all the people. And each day the
Lord added to their fellowship those who were being saved.*
(Acts 2:46-47, NLT)

As the scripture passage above states, the believers were
together each day building up one another's faith. We need
to be in Bible discussion often.

To help youth prepare for a lifetime of biblical study,
we teach them a simple format of personal Bible Study. The
study format can be used individually, as well as with small
groups, and/or with large groups of people.

One of the commonly known formats we have adopted
is called SOAP, which stands for Scripture, Observations,
Applications, and Prayer.

The form is self-explanatory, and a Bible study might be structured like this...

1. Give students a SOAP sheet.

2. Provide them with a scripture passage to study. (several verses for shorter studies, chapters for longer studies)

3. Have everyone in the group turn to the first page of the book being studied and read through the vital statistics. (Who is the author, when, to whom and why was the book written?)

4. Set a time for returning to the group and say a sending off prayer.

5. Send youth off for a time of personal reading, reflection, and filling out the SOAP sheet.

6. Once back together, a facilitator walks the group through the sheet asking students to share the thoughts they had written down under Observations.

7. Then have the group share and discuss written applications.

8. End with prayer.

One of the beauties of the SOAP format is that the leader can determine the length of time allocated for the study. We have used this model with middle school students giving them two or three verses. The format then is five minutes to fill out the sheet followed by five minutes of discussion, a quick ending prayer and the entire experience can take less than 15 minutes. Likewise, with high school students, the experience can take up to 90 minutes (five minute introduction, 30 minute personal study, and 45 minute discussion time and then ten minutes for prayer).

After a personal study or group discussion, students place their completed SOAP sheets in a notebook. As students continue to do Bible studies throughout their teen years, their notebook will continue to grow. Then, when students are older, they will find they have a notebook full of Bible studies they can read for reflection and/or can be used to facilitate a Bible study with others. Imagine having a notebook of ten, or 20, or 50 previously completed SOAP sheets. This will greatly increase the confidence of a young person to facilitate a future Bible study. Having developed good Bible Study Habits is a Faith Stone most certainly worth having in one's Faith Bag.

An example of an "SOAP Sheet"
can be found in the appendix

Faith Stone 5

Do Acts 1:8 Service

The Acts 1:8 Concept

Once children and youth have a basic understanding that we live in a broken world and that God has chosen to work through us to help piece this broken world back together, they want to make a difference. They are willing to get involved in meaningful service to others. We needed a concept that made the idea of service practical, achievable, and measurable, and we found an applicable framework in Acts 1:8.

"But you will receive power when the Holy Spirit comes upon you. And you will be my witnesses, telling people about me everywhere—in Jerusalem, throughout Judea, in Samaria, and to the ends of the earth." (Acts 1:8, NIV)

The verse describes a geographical progression of spreading the Gospel. It starts with the local city of Jerusalem. It then reaches out to the province of Judea. Next it tells of spreading God's word to the region of Samaria which extended north of Judea. Finally, it mentions the need to spread God's word to the uttermost parts of the earth.

We call it the Acts 1:8 Concept and we use it as a model for service for others. We have attached specific and current geographical areas to each of the four territories mentioned in Acts 1:8. For example, for us living in central Ohio, the verse can be interpreted this way...

Jerusalem pertains to our congregational members
Judea is central Ohio
Samaria is the United States
The uttermost parts of the earth are beyond the U.S. borders

Our desire would be for everyone in our congregation to be able to look back on the past twelve months and identify at least one ministry in which he or she participated in each of the four geographical areas.

For **Jerusalem,** we ask youth to be involved in a ministry within our own walls and/or to our own church members. Examples include...

- helping with a weekly club for children
- helping with an aspect of the worship services (read, greet, acolyte, nursery)
- being involved in the puppet ministry
- helping with Sunday School
- helping with Vacation Bible School
- visiting our members in the local assisted care facility
- being on a music team (bells, contemporary worship, choir)
- volunteering to help in the church office
- going Christmas caroling to our homebound members
- getting involved in the church picnic or another fellowship opportunity
- helping with Easter Family Fun Night
- helping with our Maundy Thursday Family Worship

- helping with the October Trunk or Treat event
- helping with our Shrove Tuesday celebration
- taking on a responsibility for an event designed for their age group

Most congregations have plenty of opportunities to serve within the walls of their church building. What might some of yours be? Do any of your service opportunities allow for youth to participate in an active way? If not, how can you enhance that culture to involve more youth?

Our **Judea** is central Ohio. These are all projects that benefit people in our community who are not members of our congregation. We offer such opportunities as...

- serving at Faith Mission (a local soup kitchen)
- serving at First English (an inner city congregation in Columbus that serves community meals every Thursday evening)
- working with the Bike Project (purchase, assemble and deliver bikes to children in local foster care)
- helping at the Re-Store (a second hand store for those in need)
- serving at the Mid-Ohio Food Bank
- leading SouperBowl Sunday
- participating in the Grove City Church Community Service Day
- participating in St. John's Awareness (local parades, community booths, etc...)
- donating clothes through the Salvation Army clothing drive
- helping with the Bed Brigade (a ministry of building and delivering beds to those in need)
- helping with the local food pantry
- helping with Habitat for Humanity
- visiting the local assisted care facility

Samaria is the United States. We give folks the opportunity to serve by giving money towards, praying for, or attending...

- a summer service trip experience outside of central Ohio
- a Denominational Social Service activity
- a Denominational Disaster Response project
- a project like the Southeast Ohio Donation Relief (delivering items to a distribution center for victims of severe weather)
- a project like Relay for Life

The Ends of the Earth is beyond our country's borders. We have opportunities such as...

- partnering with a ministry called The Genesis International Orphanage Foundation (For many years now, we've sent a group from our church on a short term mission trip to Mexico to work with the children. These children come from a local orphanage and have the opportunity to leave the orphanage and spend one beautiful week away in a camp setting with their family from the USA – that's us. In addition to our annual trip, we occasionally send educational and medical supplies and on one occasion, we sent over 300 pairs of Libby's shoes.)
- giving money or writing to a sponsored child through a faith-based organization
- getting involved in a churchwide gift project to an impoverished nation (purchasing blankets, medical supplies, food, or clothing)
- getting involved in a Heifer International type of project
- sending Christmas boxes overseas through Operation Christmas Child

- raising funds to enable an overseas village to dig a well or develop a water purification system
- purchasing protective netting for families living in mosquito infested areas overseas

As a result of the Acts 1:8 Concept, we are hoping that youth become well-rounded in their ministry of service. Even if a young person develops a passion for one particular ministry, we still feel it is important for him or her to be involved in all four aspects of Acts 1:8.

Our youth need to develop a regular ongoing discipline of service to others and Acts 1:8 gives us the framework for achieving that goal. Once youth get a taste of service, they tend to want to help again and again. Acts 1:8 has also helped to shape the outreach and support efforts of our entire congregation.

I tell parents of the youth in our congregation, "One of my goals is to take your children wherever we need to take them in order to break their hearts by the situations that break the heart of Jesus. That may be soup kitchens, homeless shelters, food pantries, assisted care facilities, children's homes, etc." I find that youth respond compassionately when they are exposed to the hurts and pains of this world. They thrive when given the opportunity to be the hands of Jesus.

In my classroom, there is a service project table. On that table, there are always a variety of service project signup sheets. Most of the clipboards have a waiting list. Once youth realize that the God of the universe has chosen to work through them to help piece this broken world back together, they step forward to fill the opportunities set before them.

Leah is thirteen years old. As long as Leah can remember, her family has gone to a local soup kitchen to provide a meal for the homeless. Several times a year, Leah would watch her dad and older siblings head off to serve sandwiches and soup to some hungry strangers. Leah couldn't wait until she was old enough to go along with her family.

Leah has now been going to the soup kitchen, multiple times a year for the past couple of years. Leah has had her heart broken by the experience. She sees the hurt and pain of hunger and homelessness. Working together, her church and her family have given her an opportunity to make a difference in this world. Leah IS making a difference, and she loves it. Serving has become a natural way of life for her. What a great experience to have with your family, to serve side by side with your mom, dad, and your brothers and sisters. Serving has drawn them closer together. I am confident Leah will be involved in some type of service to others for her entire life.

Serving is more than just a Faith Stone to have in one's Faith Bag. It is what Jesus did.

"Just as the Son of Man did not come to be served, but to serve, and to give his life as a ransom for many." (Matthew 20:28, NLT)

Faith Stone 6

Understand the Christian View of Finances

Money is an important subject. It is often said that Jesus spoke more about money than any other topic. There are all sorts of opinions about money and, in a church context; money is often a source of heightened anxiety and tension. Yet, I believe it is a topic that must be discussed with young people, and therefore congregations would be prudent to develop a plan and provide resources and opportunities to help parents lay a biblically-based financial foundation with their children.

My initial intention is for youth to gain a basic understanding of God's view of money. In addition, for those that are not receiving any financial instruction at home, I want to give a basic workable model for budgeting. Then, for those with an interest, we provide opportunities to go deeper with the topic.

There are two sheets we use to help teens begin to understand what we consider to be the biblical view of finances.

With the first sheet, The Christian View of Finances, we walk youth through scripture that gives us God's view of stewardship. The goal is to build an understanding of what the Word of God says about ownership, possessions, and giving. We ask youth to tell us in their words what they think each verse or adage means, and as a result of knowing this truth, how we should live our lives.

The second sheet is called The Financial Goals and Action Sheet and is a model budget we give students to work through. This is a sheet that I created and used myself when I was younger. You may want to tweak the percentages to reflect your personal viewpoint. Each section of the sheet gives us plenty to talk about.

Throughout the years, we touch on the topic of finances in a variety of ways. Here are some other ideas you might be interested in...

Our Congregation has a connection with Crown Financial Ministries (www.crown.org). Crown Financial Ministries is a nonprofit, 501(c) (3) organization that teaches God's biblical principles of finances to people around the world. They present biblical truths relating to stewardship, ethics, and practical money management. Crown teaches through media programs including resource workbooks and software. A member of our congregation has been trained to present Crown Financial Ministry materials to parents and other interested adults.

For younger children, we utilize our Crown Financial representative, as well as a representative from a financial service organization associated with our denomination. Presenters run through a money program with elementary and intermediate school age children. Sessions are less than an hour, active in nature, and at the end, everyone gets an item that enhances the experience, such as a piggy bank. In conjunction with the session, we highlight a ministry within the congregation that children can help financially support with money of their own. We mention the opportunity to parents and some provide extra chores so children can earn money that can be given specifically towards the cause. Throughout the experience, children have fun, get a chance to give of their own money to a worthy cause, learn a discipline, begin to see themselves as the hands of Jesus being used to help mend a broken world, and they take a step towards developing a work ethic. All "good stuff" to have in their bags!

For middle school age youth, we developed a financial simulation experience called St. Johnsville. Youth blindly pick jobs, then pay taxes, vote on levies, elect a mayor, buy cars, find a place to live, give to the church, live with the satisfaction and consequences of buying or not buying insurance, and basically just "live life." They learn about some financial realities that many don't encounter until it's too late. In session one, students are 25 years old. They then age ten years every session and retire at age 65. Choices are evaluated at the end of each session. For those looking for such an experience, a simple web search on the topic of "financial games and simulations for kids" will uncover options available for use.

Likewise, for interested high school students, there are many stock market simulation experiences that can be found on the internet.

Scripture passages we use to reinforce financial learning include:

- ownership: Everything belongs to the Lord (Psalm 24:1)
- bringing Tithes to the Church (Malachi 3:10)
- honoring God with Your First Fruits (Proverbs 3:9-10)
- storing Up Treasures in Heaven (Matthew 6:19-34)
- the Rich Young Ruler (Matthew 19:16-30)
- providing for Your Family (I Timothy 5:8)
- God Loves a Cheerful Giver (II Corinthians 9:5-9)
- wealth Does Not Bring Happiness (Ecclesiastes 5:10)
- the Sacrifice of Sharing Pleases God (Hebrews 13:16)
- feeding the Poor (Proverbs 22:9)

- the Love of Money is the Root of All Evil (I Timothy 6:10)
- beware of Attempting to Get Rich Quick (Proverbs 28:20)
- borrowing and Generous Giving (Psalm 37:21)
- increasing Wealth Honestly (Psalm 62:10)

Hopefully, through our efforts, young people will discover that God wants to be an integral part of our financial lives and that helping others through financial giving is a joy and a blessing. Understanding the Christian View of Finances is a Faith Stone that is worth its weight in gold.

You should remember the words of the Lord Jesus: "It is more blessed to give than to receive." (Acts 20:35, NLT)

**Both Financial Sheets
can be found in the appendix**

Faith Stone 7

Develop a Discipline of Fasting

Then Jesus was led by the Spirit into the wilderness to be tempted there by the devil. For forty days and forty nights he fasted and became very hungry. (Matthew 4:1-2, NLT)

There are numerous examples in the New Testament when Jesus entered a time of fasting. Jesus fasted and so should we.

Fasting causes us to take the focus off ourselves and humble ourselves before God. Fasting is the voluntary denial of something for a specific time and for a specific purpose. It can be done by an individual, a family, a congregation, or a nation. It is a self-imposed opportunity to demonstrate our love for God by sharing in the sufferings of Christ.

Notice in the following scripture that Jesus says, "When you fast." Evidently, we are expected to fast and for good reason.

"When you fast, do not look somber as the hypocrites do, for they disfigure their faces to show others they are fasting. Truly I tell you, they have received their reward in full. But when you fast, put oil on your head and wash your face, so that it will not be obvious to others that you are fasting,

but only to your Father, who is unseen; and your Father, who sees what is done in secret, will reward you." (Matthew 6:16-18, NIV)

Although the examples of fasting in the Bible are too numerous to mention, here are some of the reasons the people of God fasted.

- for Safety: Ezra fasted for safe travel. (Ezra 8:21-23)
- for Health: David fasted for the health of his child. (II Samuel 12:15-19)
- for Repentance: Joel tells us to return to the Lord with fasting. (Joel 2:12-15)
- during Mourning: The nation of Israel wept and fasted as a result of the death of Saul and his son Jonathan. (II Samuel 1:12)
- regular Routine: Leviticus talks about fasting on Holy Days. i.e. the Day of Atonement (Leviticus 23:27)
- before Making Important Decisions: In the book of Acts, believers fasted and prayed before choosing leaders. (Acts 13:2-3; 14:23)
- to Combat Evil: Jesus told the disciples that there were things that would not happen in this world without fasting and prayer. (Matthew 17:21)
- in Preparation for Upcoming Temptations: Jesus fasted in the wilderness for forty days to prepare for upcoming temptations. (Matthew 4:1-9)
- Jesus Expects Us to Fast: In the Sermon on the Mount, Jesus said, "When you fast..." (Matthew 6:16-18)

Fasting is to be a regular part of our personal faith journey. But what does that look like in the lives of young people? Our denomination embraces the liturgical calendar. As the season of Lent approaches, we explain to youth the meaning of Lent, Easter, and the importance of fasting. During this time, we encourage youth to walk along side Jesus for 40 days and share in His sufferings. As Jesus journeys toward the cross, we remind youth of the sacrifice Christ made for us. During this time we share with them some of the biblical examples of fasting, discuss what Jesus went through on the cross on our behalf, and why we as adults fast.

I tell youth, "I love Jesus so much that I am willing to give up something really important to me, to show Jesus how much I love him. Would you consider joining me?" As a result of this six week love experience, we hope students will understand that sacrifice and love go hand-in-hand and also develop an ongoing desire for the discipline of fasting.

One high school student, after becoming aware that many people do not have a bed to sleep in, decided to give up her bed for six weeks. Yes, she slept on the floor next to her bed for the entire Lenten season. Wow, what a sacrifice! And what a witness it was for those around her as she brought awareness to the plight of those without beds while expressing her love for her Savior.

To get students thinking about their Lenten sacrifice, we share with them a handout called My Lenten Sacrifice. We ask youth to prayerfully consider what to subtract from their lives during the forty days of Lent. If they are new to the concept, we ask them to consider doing their fast for one day a week for the six weeks of Lent.

Here are some examples of fasting for the faith:

I am willing to give up...

- watching TV (or certain TV shows) or going to movies
- eating a type of food (pizza, chocolate, soda, specialty coffee, fast food, candy, snacks, etc...)

- listening to music (or listening to non-Christian music) before noon
- social Media in some form
- cell phone use for one day a week and/or from noon to 3 pm on Good Friday

After one or two Lenten seasons of a traditional fast, we ask students to broaden their understanding of sacrifice. The focus of a fast is sacrifice. Although not traditional in the sense of fasting, we ask students to also consider a sacrifice of time in their willingness to add something to their daily routine. In some cases, items added to their schedule (like devotions and service to others) leave positive impressions on youth and new habits are formed.

Here are some examples of adding something for the faith:

I am willing to add...

- a daily devotion (We give youth options to choose from)
- praying through my purpose every morning (Deut. 6:5)
- processing my day each evening with the Luke 2:52 concept
- praying through my Everyday Prayer Sheet
- reading through my Thankful List
- doing a series of service projects such as visiting an assisted care facility, homeless shelter, food pantry, or soup kitchen
- participating in a hands-on work project around the church or for a neighbor
- giving a percentage of my finances for the work of the church

We start off the Lenten journey in our congregation with a party. It's called "Shrove Tuesday" or "Fat Tuesday". This is also known as Mardi Gras, which is French for "Fat Tuesday"). Shrove Tuesday is the day before Ash Wednesday, which marks the beginning of Lent. We all gather at the church for a giant pancake party. It is a festive atmosphere. We normally have over 300 people in attendance. It is the last hoorah before we settle into the discipline of fasting during Lent.

Why a pancake party? Pancakes are associated with Shrove Tuesday because they were a way to use up rich food ingredients such as yeast, eggs, milk, and sugar before the fasting season of Lent. Traditionally, fasting meant eating plainer food and refraining from food that would give pleasure. In many cultures that would mean no meat, dairy, eggs, or sugar.

In our congregation, we broaden out the festival and the fasting beyond pancakes. For the few days before the pancake party, we encourage youth to "indulge" within reason, whatever they plan to give up for the Lenten season. Enjoy that last slice of pizza, drink that extra can of soda, eat lots of chocolate, don't forget the ice cream, listen to a ceremonial last song, or watch a last TV episode. Celebrate big time! But then follow through with your commitment to give up the item in some way for the next six weeks.

The middle school students tend to start out by making a commitment to eliminate some type of food from their diet. And yes, we know six weeks can be a long time for young people to go without a favorite food (or activity). Thus, we walk with youth during this fast. We fast along with them. We enter into discussion as they experience both successes and failures in their fasting commitments. As we walk through the Lenten six weeks, our faith community is strengthened. Together, we count down the days to Easter.

Easter then becomes a HUGE celebration of the risen Christ and also the enduring of the fast. Through the experience, students realize that not only can they actually go without something for a period of time, but they learn a method of how to go about changing a habit. In some cases, youth never go back to the item they gave up, or they limit how often they indulge and they are healthier for it.

The overall concept plays well with young people and many youth participate. Some wake up Easter morning celebrating the success of their fast. Others limp across the finish line struggling with the realities of breaking the fast several times along the way. Regardless, whether youth make it through the entire six weeks maintaining their individual fast or not, it becomes a great lesson in commitment, perseverance, and faith development.

In Matthew Chapter 6, Jesus tells us, "When you fast..." Throughout scripture we see examples of fasting for repentance, safety, health, during times of mourning, to overcome temptations, and to combat evil. Fasting certainly sounds like a discipline we should all have in our Faith Bag. It also sounds like a skill that develops over time. Let's help our young people begin to develop this all important Faith Stone modeled by Jesus.

The "My Lenten Sacrifice" handout
can be found in the appendix

Faith Stones 8–22

Personal Growth and People Skills

⟡

Our faith is all about relationships–relationships with others, ourselves, and our God. It makes sense that we focus on helping youth grow in all three of these areas. The spiritual disciplines in the previous section focused mainly on our relationship with our Creator.

In this section we will discuss equipping youth with assets that will benefit their relationship with themselves and others. These Faith Stones will help youth grow in self-awareness, achieve personal growth, and gain people skills.

The goal is to lay a foundation for a biblically based self-esteem. Once established, youth can then relate better to others as they continue to develop a foundation of faith.

Personal Growth and People Skills

Faith Stone 8

Learn Intentional Relationship Building Skills

In my office, there are various wall hangings. The framed item that is highest and most strategically placed above all the other wall hangings simply states, "Relationships are more important than anything else."

We train our volunteers to understand that developing and maintaining a positive relationship with young people, based on mutual respect, is the prime directive. It's more important than who wins or loses, who gets there first, who gets the last cookie, who answers the question, etc. As youth grow into adulthood, it means that maintaining healthy relationships is more important than winning a petty political or religious argument, bickering over church scheduling conflicts, or fussing over which church group did not clean up after themselves.

We simply want to provide an environment where young people feel loved, accepted, safe, and secure. Likewise, we all know that young people need constant direction or redirection. Even when confronting inappropriate behavior, we want to connect with children and youth in a loving, respectful way.

We want to enter a relationship with children and youth as the Apostle Paul outlines in I Thessalonians 2. That is, we want to care for children and youth as a nursing mother cares for her child, loving them so much we not only share the Good News of the Gospel but we want to share our very own lives, as well. Likewise, we want to treat children and youth as a father treats his own children. We aim to urge, encourage, and exhort them to live a life that is pleasing to God.

Our thinking is that healthy relationships help build the foundation of the Christian faith. We want children and youth to have a healthy relationship with themselves, their Creator, and those with whom they come in contact. So, if enhancing faith happens through relationships, then we want students to have a skill specifically designed to enable them to begin and maintain a relationship. Our adults are trained to model it, but we need our youth to actively learn relationship skills they can use every day.

Conversation is one of those skills often overlooked. If our discipleship is based upon relationships, then we should become experts at initiating and carrying on conversations so that relationships can be built and maintained.

We have discovered that once youth have learned and practiced how to initiate and carry on a conversation with others, their confidence level is noticeably higher. Having a skill for building relationships makes entering into those various social and professional situations for the rest of their lives more comfortable. And that's a big deal!

There are several methods available to help young people (and volunteers) to develop relationship building skills. We have chosen to use a simple relationship building memorization technique taught to us by an old friend who is an expert in this area.

This method helps people organize their conversation around familiar areas of discussion; such as their name, where they live, family, where they spend their time (in school, at work, or elsewhere), hobbies and interests, travel, etc. Participants are taught how to ask good questions and are reminded of the difference between open-ended and closed-ended questions. Participants are trained to ask open-ended questions by beginning them with the words *who, what, when, where, why,* and *how* or by starting with the phrase, "Tell me about..."

This Faith Stone is hard to translate on paper. Please contact me if you would like to learn more about this simple yet excellent method for training children and youth to initiate and maintain a conversation with others.

When I met Beth, she was a quiet young lady who was a freshman in high school. One thing Beth dreaded more than anything else was getting on the school bus every morning. You see, Beth was nearly the last person to get on the bus. Each bus seat already had two people comfortably sitting there. Adding a third person to the seat would make the twenty minute ride to school really tight and uncomfortable. Beth would get on the bus each morning and lament as she slowly walked down the aisle, having to decide who she was going to inconvenience today.

Beth was a church kid. She had grown up in the church, and her family faithfully attended activities. It was no surprise when I offered a church activity, where we planned to pass on some faith skills to the group, Beth was there. For the most part, it was your typical youth group event. The only difference was I had incorporated teaching a Building Relationship skill during the mixer/game time.

About a month later, I had a very excited Beth come up to me on a Sunday morning. She explained that she had taken the faith skill I had shown her and she was using it during her morning bus ride. For several weeks, she had sat each day with someone different on the bus and had used her new Building Relationship skill with the person sitting next to her. She ended by saying that as a result of using her newly acquired skill, she had made a bunch of new friends and several of them now welcomed her sitting with them when she got on the bus. Beth now has a building relationship stone in her bag, one that will help her to slay the giants of uncomfortable social situations.

It was a simple skill that took about twenty minutes to learn, yet it had profoundly affected her life in a positive way. That's what acquiring Faith Stones can do for people and is why I have devoted my life to passing them on to anyone that has an interest. Again, if this is a faith skill you would like to ingrain in your youth culture, please contact me. It's definitely a worthy stone to have in one's Faith Bag.

Faith Stone 9

Develop a Supportive Faith Web

We call it "Faith Webbing."

Our vision in our congregation is to "wrap children and youth in a web of faith so loving and caring that they will know Christ and always want to be a part of a local congregation and its mission."

We have been developing the Faith Webbing concept in our congregation for over 30 years. We started with a philosophy called "relational ministry." The goal was to have youth leaders at events that did not have any programming responsibilities. These caring adults were simply present to be "relational" with young people. They were there to build friendships with children and youth with the hopes that those relationships would point children and youth to Christ.

In some congregations, this relational ministry approach is a youth leader going to school functions or to a community event or taking a couple of teens out to a restaurant for the sole purpose of building relationships. This relationship did prove important in the life of the young person; although, sometimes it was the only significant connection to the church. If the youth leader became occupied with the busyness and demands of ministry, then the connection weakened. Worse yet, if the youth leader moved on, then the connection with the church was regrettably broken.

Faith Webbing is a much deeper and more purposeful approach to connecting youth to the church. Its premise is to intentionally identify relationship voids in young peoples' lives and then fill those voids with church members of the needed ages. A young person is then surrounded by numerous faith walks that they can emulate. Little is random, accidental, or left to chance. Relationships are prayerfully, purposively, and intentionally sought, built, and sustained.

The end result of this approach to ministry is that youth get to know scores of people of all ages within the congregation. They get to know these folks in a safe, fun, loving, and faith nurturing environment. As this occurs, the church then becomes a place of deep meaningful relationships.

For some youth, there might not be a parent, grandparent, aunt, uncle, older sibling, or younger sibling in their life. In Faith Webbing, we deliberately identify those relational voids and then aim to fill those relationship needs with loving, caring people from within the congregation. It is common for youth to develop "grandparent relationships" with several of the older members. Thus, the church becomes a place where youth develop needed surrogate relationships.

We introduce the Faith Webbing concept to children and youth in various ways. Our focus with the elementary school age children is on the leadership team. We explain the concept to the adult and teen leaders during training sessions. As leaders catch the vision for Faith Webbing, we know our children will be surrounded with lots of faith relationships. We aspire to have a healthy ratio of children to leaders at events. With the younger ages we hope for at least a 2:1 ratio. With older youth we strive for a 3:1 ratio of youth to adults. The leaders understand that they are there to intentionally build faith relationships with children. Together, we purposely love kids into the kingdom.

When youth get older, we offer specific Faith Webbing sessions. In these sessions, youth get the opportunity to begin to define their personal Faith Web. They contemplate who is in their Faith Web and who needs to be in their web. We talk about the quality traits we see in the people in their Faith Web. We plant the seed that youth can develop these qualities in their lives and also be on someone else's Faith Web. As this exercise is revisited, youth appreciate the people God has placed in their lives, they are reminded that they are not alone in their faith walk, and they are encouraged to reach out and develop more Faith Web relationships.

This exercise becomes a springboard for deepening relationships and a place to recognize relationship voids. Our mission jumps from sharing the vision to connecting people. We become attentive to relationship needs and prayerfully seek to weave people together in a faith-based environment. God is the supreme Faith Weaver. We are privileged to be the vehicle through which He weaves.

Ultimately, youth become engaged with people of all ages. These relationships lead to them becoming involved in the life and mission of the church. No longer are children and youth separated from the congregation and expected to meet with just their age group, in a room set aside specifically for them, apart from the rest of the congregation. As youth see folks in their Faith Web living out their faith, youth get a vision of how they can be active in serving others, often working alongside those in their Faith Web.

Below is an example of an introductory Faith Webbing session.

On one occasion, we intentionally introduced the Faith Webbing concept to a group of high school youth. About forty of us were away on a weeklong, faith-based, skills training experience. We gave each high school student a poster size post-it note with his or her name placed in the middle of the sheet. We asked each person to create a web of names of people in our congregation whose faith they admired. We gave them numerical goals. We told them to list six grandparent age people from our congregation, six people who were of parental age, six people in their twenties, six peers, and yes, six people younger than themselves, all whose faith they admired.

It was fascinating to see their minds begin to work. We gave them hints...think of Sunday school teachers, VBS teachers, music leaders, Weekly Club leaders, people you've heard speak at church, etc. The teens worked on their Faith Web sheets a little each day. Near the end of the week, they took turns presenting their Faith Web posters to the group.

Adelyn was one of the first teens to present her work of art, as she found the exercise an exciting opportunity to document her relationships. Remember, we ask the youth to list up to 30 people in their webs. Well, Adelyn could have talked for 30 minutes. You see, Adelyn is one of those "church kids." Her mom went to church, her dad went to church, her brother went to church, her grandparents went to church, her aunts, uncles, cousins, you name it...they were in church each Sunday. She had been baptized in the church, confirmed in the church; she will probably marry in the church. Yep, Adelyn was not just a church kid...she was a St. John's kid.

Without knowing the concept, Adelyn had been building her web of faith her entire life. She had 50+ names on her poster sized post-it note and was still adding names as she was giving her presentation—names of both family and non-family members within the congregation. How fun!

What's the benefit? The benefit is that you never had to worry about Adelyn. If Adelyn had missed three weeks of church in a row, a dozen people would have been tracking her down. To her, Sunday morning was a giant church family reunion where she could come and bebop around, making connections with scores of people she loves and admires and who love and admire her. It is a perfect faith building scenario.

Want a greater benefit? All those years of being in the church building several times a week really paid off. By the time Adelyn was a teen, she had a rock solid faith foundation that was unshakable. Now, as the Apostle Paul wrote in I Corinthians 3:2, she was ready to move beyond milk and get into the meatier portion of the faith. To Adelyn, seeking God's calling was second nature. What a joy it is to spend time with a mature spiritual teen of God.

Then there was Eric. Eric was a young man who had a difficult family situation. He ended up living with a stepfather who did not take much interest in him. To Eric's credit, he stayed involved in the church. He went to weekly activities and on summer church trips. He attended the same experiences as Adelyn, but Eric's Faith Web looked very different. There were no family members included and most of the names listed were people who were in the room at the time. There were holes in his Faith Web just about everywhere.

Fortunately, Eric hung with us through his high school years. This gave us the opportunity to connect him with various people in the congregation that he needed to know. Our ministry to Eric had focus and intentionality. Our goal for Eric became a paraphrase of our church vision; to surround Eric in a web of faith so loving and caring that he would know Jesus, develop meaningful church family relationships, and keep him connected to scores of faith-based people.

During his high school years, Eric developed good friendships, got connected with parent age members that treated him like a nephew, and he ended up with caring grandparent age people in his life. His web was constantly being developed.

Now in his late twenties, Eric has a daughter of his own. I recently had a conversation with Eric when he picked up his daughter from Vacation Bible School. He commented how much the church has meant to him over the years. He also mentioned how he progressed from being a teen helper at Vacation Bible School, to leading portions of the program as a college student, to now bringing his preschool school age daughter to VBS. It is exciting to see Eric's commitment to bringing her to church and to see his daughter making Faith Web connections at such a young age.

God bless all those people who opened up their hearts, lives, and homes to an "at risk" teen who needed to be shown the love and grace of God through a caring congregation.

Understanding the concept of Faith Webbing and having the ability to build a web of faith around yourself and your family is a Faith Stone that is, well, priceless.

> For more on this concept, acquire the book
> "Faith Webbing" (Xulon Press)

Faith Stone 10

Know What You Believe

I invited an older gentleman named Paul to visit our youth group and share about his faith. His talk was simple, to the point, but effective. Paul loved the Lord, and he embraced the Apostles' Creed and its importance. He emphasized the Creed as the written work that holds us together. He even went so far as to say that the Creed is probably the only thing that those of us in this room would all agree upon. Because of our belief in the elements of the Creed, we could disagree on everything else and still hold hands in faith. Good words, good message, and easy for youth to understand.

A creed is a belief statement. The Apostles' Creed is a corporate belief statement that we recite regularly because it contains the foundational beliefs of our faith. It forms us. It provides common ground. It holds us together.

As the young people in our congregation move toward confirmation, we believe it is helpful for them to write out a statement of their developing faith. We ask each student to write a personal "I Believe" statement or personal creed of faith.

In our system, it is a statement that takes a year to develop. We start in the fall of their eighth grade year at a session called the Apostles' Creed Learning Event. Each student is

handed a sheet of paper with the words "I Believe..." printed
20 times down the left side of the page. We simply ask students to complete the sentence all 20 times. We give them
some ideas to help them get started and ask that they write
one sentence about such topics as:

God the Father	God the Son
God the Holy Spirit	Forgiveness
Mercy	Salvation
Grace	Redemption
God's Love	Heaven
Eternal Life	Baptism
Communion	Prayer
The Word of God	Service to Others
Purpose in Life	Truth
Assurance	Blessings
Covenant	Faith
Future	Gifts
Guidance	Protection
Holiness	Mission
Perseverance	Responsibility
Righteousness	Thanksgiving

Students are also encouraged to page through their Bibles
and the concordance in the back of their Bibles (or use their
phones to search the web) for topics and ideas. Youth often
times end up incorporating scripture into their statement by
paraphrasing a verse such as...

- I have been saved by grace through faith
- I believe I can do all things through Christ who
  strengthens me
- I have been created to do good works
- the Lord will direct my steps all the days of my life
- I believe I am a joint-heir with Jesus Christ

Lines from favorite faith-based songs also show up in the statements of youth...

- God the Father is my strong tower, a refuge over me
- I am an over-comer through Jesus
- my life is not my own and I will not be shaken
- step by step He leads me and I will follow Him all of my days
- the God of angel armies is always by my side

When students have completed the assignment, we collect the sheets, copy them, and return the original to the student. We keep the copy for future use. Youth are asked to consider adding to their list on their own in the upcoming months.

Five months later, we hold our annual eighth grade Faith Advance (a time when we pull students together to specifically work on faith development). Part of the time at the Advance is spent further developing each student's "I Believe" statement. Students are given back the work that was collected the previous fall. We do a quick overview of the Apostles' Creed, give the students an opportunity to add to the sentences they had written, and then we take the next step of putting it together. Students look at the sentences before them and begin to group them into four categories: God the Father, God the Son, God the Holy Spirit, and Service/Purpose. As a result, paragraphs begin to form. The work is again copied, originals distributed, and the copies filed away for future use.

Several months later, we pull out the work again. This time students read through the paragraphs they started at the Advance. Excess words and topics are removed. Paragraphs are more clearly defined, and an "I Believe" statement emerges.

Once more, a few weeks later, the work is again refined. Students are given the opportunity to revisit their statements and make final changes. The final draft is reviewed by the Pastor for a theology check and students are given the opportunity to read their statements out loud. We want students to be comfortable expressing their faith before the big day when they profess their faith in front of many witnesses.

On confirmation day, during a worship service, students are invited to affirm their baptism. During this time, youth publically share their "I Believe" statement and confirm their faith in the Triune God. After sharing his or her personal statement of faith, the student kneels, several people lay hands on the student, a specially chosen verse is read, a prayer is said, a bell in the bell tower rings specifically for him or her with a loud resounding "Amen," and parents and grandparents shed tears of joy. My wife will tell you that she can hear the heavens rejoicing, on this particular morning, as students give witness to their faith.

As David daily guarded the sheep, he never knew when he would encounter a threat. His shepherd's bag had to be constantly with him. His tested skills had to be ready at a moment's notice to combat evil. What reassurance it must have been to David to have skills to go along with his deep faith. In today's society, our youth encounter threats to their faith all throughout the day. There are threats that try to change a student's belief system or, in the brokenness of life, cause doubt in their minds. There are the threats of an unknown future that plants seeds of fear. Having sure knowledge of God can replace lies, doubt, and fear with confidence, trust, and hope. Having a personal "I Believe" statement is one of the most important assets the church can impart to a young person. Walking through a yearlong process of writing a statement of faith helps youth to solidify their beliefs, and it's an essential Faith Stone to have in their Faith Bag. Way cool!

Faith Stone 11

Know Your Standards

There once was a boy named Jasper. When he was little, Jasper and his dad would go and watch his uncle coach football. There was nothing quite like the excitement of a Saturday afternoon collegiate football game–sitting in the stands, eating hot dogs, and cheering on the team.

One day, watching from the stands, Jasper saw his uncle walk over to a guy on the sidelines who was holding a clipboard. They talked for a few seconds. Then his uncle pulled a football player aside, said something to the player, patted him on the back, and sent the player running onto the field. This player then said something to the quarterback, and the game continued. Not knowing the guy with the clipboard, Jasper watched his uncle throughout the game. Time after time, his uncle would talk to this guy on the sidelines.

By the end of the fourth quarter, the team was down by four points. They had the ball on the two-yard line with only seconds left on the clock. The situation looked intense. The crowd was on the edge of their seat. Jasper anxiously watched as his uncle once again talked to the guy with the clipboard and then motioned to the quarterback. The team lined up. His uncle looked calm. The clock started to tick down. The ball snapped…the crowd cheered…Jasper jumped up and down…his team had won! After the lights had dimmed and everyone had gone home, Jasper was left pondering, "Just who was that guy with the clipboard?"

Before most football games, all the possible offensive plays for every possible situation are already decided upon and written down on a chart. Coaches already know what plays their team is prepared to run when it is second down and a short amount of yardage to gain, as well as on fourth down and a long way to go. All of the scenarios are carefully thought through beforehand. The guy next to Jasper's uncle had a clipboard listing all of the plays and scenarios the team was prepared to run. This helped the coach make good, logical decisions during otherwise emotional times.

Having advance written plans for encountering the various perceived situations takes the emotion out of the decision-making process and enables coaches to make better decisions. It greatly reduces the odds of making poor decisions in the heat of a situation.

The San Francisco 49ers Super Bowl teams of the 1980s actually scripted their first 17 plays each week. These plays were determined early in the week and practiced over and over again. Everyone was prepared; every scenario was thought through.

Likewise, when you are in a situation where you have to make a quick decision, or one packed with emotion, it is important to think through, ahead of time, what you are going to do in that situation. For example, what will you do if you find yourself at a party where something going on is making you uncomfortable? Or what will you do if you find yourself in a situation with your peers and they are about to do something illegal, immoral, or unethical? Developing some basic standards to live by can help you make better decisions.

Below is a tool I use to help young people to develop some standards to live by; in essence it is their "clipboard." Standards are typically one line sentences, which describe criteria for moral conduct of what one will or will not do in a particularly challenging time. I encourage youth to develop a dozen or so written standards and to revisit them often.

Examples:

In the area of: *Character Development*
My standard is...   *To be honest and have integrity in all my dealings with people*

In the area of: *Relationships*
My standard is...   *To affirm others and strive to bring out the "best" in them*

In the area of: *Sports*
My standard is...   *To win with humility and to lose with dignity*

In the area of: *Humor*
My standard is...   *To not participate in humor at the expense of others*

You get the idea. I also want to be clear that my job is to make sure that youth have standards. It is not to tell them what standards to have. I am careful not to impose my standards on them. I tend to share only two or three of my standards and even then I pick standards to share that are rather generic in nature, like the examples above. After a few minutes of time alone writing out personal standards, a group discussion takes place. During this time I have the opportunity to reinforce good topics and good standards written by their peers.

I especially like parents to be present at this session. After time alone, parents and their children gather together throughout the room to share what standards they initially wrote down. What a privilege it is to give parents and children an opportunity to work on written standards together. Joshua 24:15 states, "As for me and my house, we will serve the Lord." This session gives parents an easy, comfortable atmosphere to have an open discussion with their child (children) on the standards they may have for their household.

I like to begin a session such as this by brainstorming together areas where they could have a written standard to live by (drugs, alcohol, dating, attire, relationships, entertainment, social media, confidentiality, church attendance, language, health and fitness, homework, sports, music, technology, etc.). In the first session, participants develop just two to four standards. Eventually, they increase the number to a dozen or so written Standards to Live By.

If you're looking for a good introduction into standards, a good place to start is to review the Ten Commandments. The Ten Commandments give students (and you and me) standards for holy living. With youth, we compare the Ten Commandments to a fence and a mirror. A fence is a boundary that keeps children within it safe but also gives them freedom to run and play. A mirror reflects back to us our image and what we look like and if we need to make any suitable changes to our appearance. Along with the Ten Commandments, we also search the scriptures for direction for holy living. Over time, we do sessions encouraging students to attach specific Bible verses to each standard.

Example:

In the area of: _Language_
My standard is... _To say only positive things about others_

*Do not let any unwholesome talk come out of your mouths,
but only what is helpful for building others up according to
their needs, that it may benefit those who listen. (Ephesians
4:29, NIV)*

We all have standards; however, there is something about
writing them down and reviewing them regularly that embla-
zons standards in our brains. Then, as situations come up
throughout the day, standards will come to mind to remind
us of the parameters that we have set on our behavior.

Having written standards to live by is a tremendous item
to have in one's Faith Bag. It is like having your own guy
with a clipboard to go to when the game gets intense. I do
it; it works!

*So you must live as God's obedient children. Don't slip back
into your old ways of living to satisfy your own desires. You
didn't know any better then. But now you must be holy in
everything you do, just as God who chose you is holy. For
the Scriptures say, "You must be holy because I am holy."*
(I Peter 1:14-16, NLT)

> Gary enjoys nothing more than helping
> parents and children together develop
> written standards to live by

Faith Stone 12

Know Your Mission

———————

During a session for high school students when we introduced the concept of having a personal mission and
direction, a young lady named Megan was in attendance. At
the session, she thought long and hard but could only come
up with one word, "Hebrew." That was it. I asked her why
she wrote the word "Hebrew," and she said she did not know.
It just came to her. I wasn't sure where to go with the discussion from there, so I just smiled and accepted her thought.

When Megan was a young girl, she had come to under-
stand that Jesus was Jewish. Having a love for her faith
and Savior, she became interested in the Jewish culture.
Ironically, a Messianic Jew was a part of our congregation.
Megan became interested in his heritage and a friendship
formed between him and Megan's family. Through him,
Megan began to learn about the culture and traditions of the
Hebrew people.

So, it actually made sense that Megan would write down
the word "Hebrew" during the session on mission and direction. Then, as we revisited the concept of mission and direction through her high school years, Megan began to put
further thought into her interest in the Hebrew people. She
learned about the Jewish Festivals and even had her family

practice a couple of them at home. Wanting to gain a fuller understanding of scripture, she set goals to become fluent in both Greek and Hebrew.

In college, Megan was required to do volunteer work in the community. She was given a list of places she could volunteer. She immediately chose the Jewish Community Center. She soon found herself spending time in both the Jewish and non-Jewish communities. In her quest to explain her interests to her friends and family, she found herself becoming a bridge to help the two faith traditions understand each other.

Megan is now ten years beyond high school. She has an understanding of Hebrew and soon plans to start her study of Greek. She finds herself attending a messianic congregation. A messianic congregation is a blend of evangelical Christian theology with elements of religious Jewish practice and terminology. Messianic Judaism holds the belief that Jesus is both the Jewish Messiah and "God the Son", and salvation is given only through acceptance of Jesus as Savior. Her particular congregation is made up of both non-Jewish and Jewish believers in Jesus. She has studied and learned the basics of both faith traditions. Part of her mission in life is to be a bridge between both Gentiles and Jews who have given their lives to Christ.

Although Megan's interest in the Hebrew people did not start during our sessions on mission and direction, they did cause Megan to focus, think, rethink, and then set some goals in what for her had become a genuine interest. That is what we are hoping to accomplish. To regularly surface the idea of mission and direction so youth have the opportunity to continue the process of asking, "Is there something in life for which I have a great passion?"

Yes, with most youth the direction changes or at least is altered. However, how wonderful it is to encourage youth to ask the question while they search and pray for God's leading in life.

I recently visited Megan's congregation. I was asked to speak to their educational team and introduce various ways to pass on the faith to their children. Megan was the host for the event. She is flourishing in her faith community. She loves her congregation, she loves the people, and she is growing in her understanding of the Jewish culture and in her relationship with Christ. Megan could not be more pleased with where God has led her. It is as if she has been specifically designed for this role in life. Megan has identified a purpose in life and has developed a personal mission that has eternal significance. How meaningful and joyous life becomes when one has those basic but important attributes of the faith figured out.

So, let's keep asking the questions of our young people, "Is there something about which you are really passionate?" "What energizes you?" "What do you do that causes you to completely lose track of time?" Then, as youth work and serve through church ministries, these questions begin to take on an eternal perspective. This often times leads to young people devoting their lives to something meaningful.

A plaque hangs in my classroom at the church. It reads, "Do not fear failure but rather fear being successful at something that does not matter."

Then there is Julie. During her middle and high school years, Julie attended many of our church activities including the leadership events. She also joined us on summer church trips, particularly our annual Leadership Academy. Julie eventually became a presenter at the Leadership Academy. Over those years, she was present for the sessions on discovering gifts and personal mission/direction. Throughout the process it was obvious Julie had a love for languages. Once we became aware of her interest we, along with her parents, were able to encourage her in developing that interest.

Julie was also an avid reader. One evening when she was a freshman in high school, we showed a short video during the learning time. At the end of the clip there was a quote displayed from C.S. Lewis. Julie leaned over and asked, "Who is C.S. Lewis?" Julie's question led to a book club being formed. The group met and talked for a couple of hours each Sunday afternoon about faith and life. We read through The Screwtape Letters, Mere Christianity, and The Great Divorce. We eventually went on to read The Hiding Place and Hinds Feet on High Places. These were powerful books that led to great discussions. They helped Julie continue to process through a direction in life. The summer after high school, Julie went on our annual mission trip to Mexico. (Our congregation sends approximately 15 people each July to lead a VBS program at a church camp dedicated to underprivileged children in Mexico.) Julie had an extraordinary experience. Her faith, her interest in languages, and a newly discovered love for travel all came together in one experience. A direction in life was formulating.

Julie went on to college and majored in Spanish while receiving a minor in French. While in college, she came across the organization Wycliffe Bible Translators. Her love for languages, travel, and desire to reach others with the Gospel was not only becoming clearer, there was now a realistic avenue for her to pursue. After college graduation and two years of training and preparation, Julie and her husband headed to Tanzania to help translate previously unwritten languages. These translations will lead to the Word of God being written down in these languages for the first time. What a powerful mission in which to devote your life! Julie and her husband have been in Tanzania for two years and plan to remain there for the foreseeable future.

Like Megan, Julie's interest did not start during our sessions on mission and direction. But also like Megan, the sessions were part of a larger scale, results-oriented strategy to help young people sift through gifts, interests, and faith. The mission and direction sessions helped Julie to continue to give attention to the bigger picture and bigger questions in life, such as "Is there something in life for which you have such a great passion that you wish to devote yourself to?"

For Julie and her husband, the answer is "yes."

So how do we start? To get students thinking about the idea of a personal mission statement, I pass out a handout of names of well-known people along with statements that are associated with them. I ask students to try to match the person with the statement. For example:

- to eradicate slavery in America *(Abraham Lincoln)*
- to love the poor and downtrodden *(Mother Teresa)*
- to lead the country out of the midst of depression *(Franklin Roosevelt)*
- to change a nation so my children will not be judged by the color of their skin but by the nature of their character *(Martin Luther King Jr.)*
- to nurse the sick, dress the wounded, and soothe the dying *(Clara Barton)*
- to invent the un-inventible by trying just one more time *(Thomas Edison)*

After talking about these well-known people, I make the point that some people get the opportunity to develop a personal mission statement or direction over time. Martin Luther King Jr. was prayerfully led into his mission. He easily could have thought of his own safety and kept silent. For others, as was the case with Abraham Lincoln and Franklin Roosevelt, their mission was thrust upon them.

Next, I use Biblical examples of personal mission statements to get things rolling.

The Apostle Paul's mission statement can be found in
Col 1:28...

• *To bring each person to maturity in Christ.*

King David might have worded his statement to read...

• *I will chase after God's own heart.* (Acts 13:22, NLT)

Samuel of the Old Testament may have simply stated...

• *Yes, Lord, your servant is listening.* (I Samuel
  3:10, NLT)

Nehemiah may have worded his statement to read...

• *to return to the land of my ancestors and to organize
  the rebuilding of the city of Jerusalem, its walls, and
  its people* (Nehemiah 2:5)

Many students use a Bible verse as their personal mission
statement or direction.

• *to conduct myself in a manner worthy of the Gospel*
  (Philippians 1:27)
• *to grow in wisdom and stature and in favor with both
  God and others* (Luke 2:52)
• *to love my neighbor as myself* (Matthew 22:39)
• *to be holy for thou art Holy* (Leviticus 19:2)
• *to be kind, tenderhearted and forgiving just as God has
  forgiven me through Christ Jesus* (Ephesians 4:32)
• *to do all for the glory of God* (I Corinthians 10:31)

Some write their own personal mission statement. They
start with an identified gift and weave it into their statement.

For example:

- *to use my musical abilities for the glory of God*
- *to use my teaching talents to bring the word of God to children and youth in an educational setting*
- *to use my interest in information technology to bring others to a deeper devotion to Christ*

Or my personal mission statement, which is, t*o train and equip God's people with the necessary faith skills to live out their personal calling in life.*

Even though it can take years to develop and is often in constant revision, the mission statement concept is a Faith Stone that gives one direction and focus in life. Even if students do not completely develop their written personal mission statements, the process is still very helpful for students to carefully think through a direction in which to head.

Faith Stone 13

Know Your Ministry Plan

In Acts, chapter 16, Paul speaks of a woman named Lydia. She is described as a dealer of purple cloth from the city of Thyatira. She heard the preaching of Paul and gave her heart to Christ. Paul goes on to say that Lydia was a worshiper of God, a willing servant who opened up her house for use by the church, and she had her entire household baptized into the faith. Lydia shared her faith with those she came in contact with through her business. Her faith permeated every aspect of her life. You could say that Lydia had a personal ministry to her friends, family, and customers. And being the business woman that she was, I bet she had intentionality to everything she did.

Most believers do not think in terms of identifying a personal ministry plan. We tend to think in terms of becoming *involved* in a ministry, not *having* a ministry. Besides, most of us lead very busy lives. Youth have school, homework, church, jobs, friends, scouts, and other extra-curricular activities. In our hectic pace, it is hard to find time to even relax. But develop a personal ministry?

In our congregation, the answer is "Yes." And actually, many of us naturally create personal ministry plans. Think about it. Anyone that sets goals for the future is creating a plan. If we simply take that plan and offer it up to the Lord, we have created a personal ministry plan. Or if we choose to intentionally live out our faith within the context of our daily activities, we have in a sense developed a personal ministry. In our congregation, what we have created is a culture where every young person is not only involved in ministry but is defining their own personal ministry.

When Mark was in high school, he was on the football team. The football team consumed much of Mark's time year-round. I spend much of my time with "church kids" in the church building. Many of the youth are in the building three or four times a week. These "church kids" attend as much as their schedules will allow; however, this would not work for Mark. Attending school and being on the football team consumed just about all of his time. Mark needed a way to have an active faith while going to school and being on the football team.

As a freshman, Mark attended the session we offered on developing a Personal Ministry Plan. Through the process, Mark identified his personal ministry to be the high school football team. When he was with the guys on the team, he felt it was his responsibility to be a good witness for Christ. Mark set his aim at practicing with all his might, being a good sport, supporting and encouraging his teammates, and striving to be Christ-like. Mark is a good example of a young person doing ministry in the community based on his interests.

Mark and I would stand up in front of a group at our church, and I would ask questions like, "Mark, do you come to our Monday night Bible study?"

He would say, "No, I don't."

I would ask, "Are you in our praise band that meets on Tuesday nights?"

"Nope," was the reply.

"Do you help with the middle school program on Wednesday evenings? Attend the high school youth group on Wednesdays? Or help with the elementary age youth group on Thursdays?"

"No, nope, and never," were his responses.

"Mark," I would say, "You are really making me look bad. What do you do with your church and faith?" Mark would then go on to explain that he came to worship, attended Sunday school, and attended our training experiences but the majority of his time was spent outside of the church building. His ministry was to the high school football team.

Mark had developed his Standards to Live By, and he had defined his Personal Ministry. His goal was to have a positive influence on the lives of the football players on his team. He actively prayed for them, he spent time with them on their turf, and he did his best to be a positive role model among those guys for the four years of high school.

By the time he was a senior, Mark was captain of the football team, and he was respected and admired by everyone. He was a great witness for Christ and a solid person. No one could have had a greater influence on the guys on his football team than Mark. He had been positioned and placed on the football team for God's glory. He lived out his faith among the team. In fact, you could say he lived out his daily Job Description while among his teammates. He was growing physically, growing spiritually, earning the respect of others, and living a life pleasing to God.

There are many ways to help students identify their very own personal ministry plan. One way that has worked for us is to ask youth to jot down

- every activity that they are involved in, and
- every place they spend their time.

Students' lists often include school, sports, music groups, school clubs, church activities, work, friends, school plays, 4-H, scouting, and family.

After students have created their lists of activities and places, we introduce the idea that each of these activities or places has a ministry aspect to it. The "I'm too busy to do ministry" excuse is no longer valid. We take the "busyness" in students' lives and help them to turn their activities into ministries. In essence, "bloom where you are planted!"

To achieve this goal, we ask students to think through each of their activities or places on their list and to consider how they might be a positive Christian influence. For example:

During the time I spend with/in: _____,

I plan to influence those I come in contact with, for the cause of Christ, by...

As youth identify areas of influence and prayerfully write down their thoughts, they begin to develop a personal ministry plan. What is particularly effective about this process is that students come up with a plan without realizing it. If you had asked them to write out a personal ministry plan, you would have likely received lots of blank stares and confused looks. However, if you ask how they can have an influence for Christ on those they come in contact with each day, they then can begin to grasp the personal ministry concept. Students learn that wherever they have been placed they can be a positive witness for Christ, which is eternal.

Here's a more detailed example:

During the time I spend in: ___*Marching Band*___,

I plan to influence those I come in contact with for the cause of Christ by...

   Doing all things without grumbling or complaining (Phil 4:14)_____

   Committing myself to only making positive statements about others_____

   Not participating in humor at the expense of others_____

   Praying for my squad, my squad leader, and my band director_____

   Taking the opportunity to invite others to something going on at church_____

I tell youth to keep it simple. There is no need to make a list of a dozen activities or places. Choose one or two areas of influence, and this becomes your personal ministry plan.

As a leader, you can quickly see how you can tie the Standards to Live By and Personal Mission sessions to this idea of identifying a Personal Ministry Plan. This is where it all begins to come together. Church now becomes a place where I can be with others going the same direction in life and a place where I can take a break from the world to reflect, refocus, recharge and become better equipped to be a good witness of Christ.

Over the years, this concept of developing personal ministry plans has reaped many benefits. It has...

- helped youth to see that it is okay to be involved in activities outside of the church

- given youth a deeper meaning for being involved in their activities
- reminded youth of the way they are to conduct themselves when they are in the community
- helped youth to see that the church is here to love and accept them while continuing to equip them for their ministry. Church attendance now has more meaning.
- helped youth to develop a prayer life centered on their ministry
- helped youth to have an influence for Christ in their world
- helped youth to understand they will always have a personal ministry through their activities beyond high school
- helped youth to grasp that the God of the universe wishes to touch the world in a positive way through them

Being able to define a personal ministry context based on who we spend our time with is a Faith Stone that both keeps us on track with our faith and helps us to be an example of what it means to be Christian. That's a powerful Faith Stone that each one of us needs to have in our Faith Bag.

> If you are affiliated with a Christian school, consider developing a strategic plan for implementing the Outcome-Based concept in your school. Gary would love to help.

Faith Stone 14

Grow Thankfulness

It is important to realize and recognize everything that we have been given. While much of the rest of the world struggles to meet the daily needs of food, clothing, and shelter, most of us do not need to concern ourselves with daily survival. In fact, most of us get to choose what and when we eat, what we wear, and, as we grow older, we will have choices of where we live, work, and vacation.

It is good for us to acknowledge what we have been given. James 1:17 reminds us "Whatever is good and perfect comes down to us from God our Father, who created all the lights in the heavens." God loves a thankful heart. One way to help our youth develop a "thankful" heart is by creating a list of things for which we are thankful.

This experience can take place in any type of room; however, I especially enjoy holding this session in a sanctuary. There is something about candles, an altar, stained glass, and the peacefulness of the room that makes it more meaningful. Outdoor settings also are good for setting a mood of thankfulness. Before starting the session, I post a dozen sheets of paper around the area. Each sheet has a reflective question written on it covering the topics of Family, Friends, Faith, Food, Possessions, The World, etc.

At the beginning of the session, I hand out a piece of paper for students to write on. This paper will become their thankful list. We read the verses on top of this paper, making the point that God desires for us to be thankful. Then, I ask students to walk, by themselves, around the room and read each posted question. They should thoughtfully answer the question while listing items they are grateful for on their sheet. To set the mood, quiet background music is played. This activity takes 15 to 20 minutes. Some students will get to all the posted topics and some will stop and linger in one place. It really does not matter, as long as youth are prayerfully working on their list.

> ## The reflective questions for this session can be found in the appendix

Sometimes this initial reflection experience can take longer than 15 minutes. Actually, it often does! It depends on the setting and mood of the group. But, at some point, when a majority of the students have either exhausted the questions in the room or they are ready for the next instruction, I gather the students back together. I go around and ask each student to share with me one thing he or she wrote on their thankful list. I continue asking until everyone has shared at least one thing they are thankful for and then I go back around and give youth the opportunity to mention other things they've listed. Some youth will mention one or two items. Some youth will want to read their entire list. Regardless, most of them have generated a solid start to their thankful list.

As students put their thankful list in a notebook or slide the paper into their Bibles, I tell them, "You have just started a list you can continue to add to in the days ahead. By the time you are a freshman in high school, you should have at least 200 items on your thankful list! Now, that's a lot to be thankful for!" Many students are already well on their way to 200 items, so it is no great stretch of the imagination that they can do it. They will accomplish the challenge easily.

Also, I give youth ideas on how to use their thankful list. I tell students, "The thankful list is a good place to start a personal prayer time. Instead of starting your personal prayer time by asking God for stuff, consider starting your prayer time by sitting quietly and mentioning one item (or person) on your thankful list to God. Then sit in silence for 20 seconds reflecting on that particular item (or person) and on God's goodness, faithfulness, and His provision."

For example:

"Lord, I thank you for my mom." (Silence)

"Lord, I thank you for my dad." (Silence)

"God, thanks for nature and spring days." (Silence)

"I thank you for your grace and forgiveness." (Silence)

I also tell students, "On those days when you are feeling discouraged and/or if you have had a bad day, pull out your thankful list and spend some time reading or praying over your list. It can be helpful in lifting your spirit to be reminded of all of the positives going on in your life."

When Kellen was in seventh grade, he attended an event similar to the activity described above and he started his thankful list. When the event was over, Kellen had close to one hundred items on his list. By the time Kellen had advanced to eighth grade, he had his list of two hundred. But Kellen did not stop there. He kept adding to his list and when he was a freshman, Kellen had over five hundred items on his thankful list. By this time, he was listing everything from his family members to chocolate, ice cream, and pizza.

Interestingly enough, during his high school years, Kellen came to the conclusion he needed to narrow down his list. This came as a result of attending a Group Workcamp mission trip. The Workcamp experience had a profound impact on Kellen. Although he was thankful for items like chocolate, ice cream, and pizza, Kellen wanted to start focusing on more purposeful things, such as running water and electricity. He narrowed his list back down to about two hundred.

By his senior year, Kellen's list began to grow again. But this time instead of adding various foods to his thankful list, he made his list deeper and more meaningful. You see, initially, Kellen wrote his mom, dad, and his brother on his list, representing each with one word. As a senior in high school, he began to expand his thankful list, and single words grew into sentences: "I am thankful for a loving family that has supported me and will continue to support me every step of my journey in life."

At the time of this writing, Kellen is motoring his way through his college years. He now spends his summers as an adult staff member for Group Workcamps. Yes, Kellen is now part of the leadership team providing Workcamp experiences to thousands of young people each summer, experiences he hopes will profoundly impact young people, just the way he was affected when he was in high school.

Kellen is a happy, amiable, and appreciative young adult. All those years of focusing intently on God, and thanking Him for His gifts, have made a difference in Kellen's life. I cannot help but think this is why Kellen has such a refreshing attitude of gratitude. And it's a Faith Stone that he will have in his Faith Bag all of his life.

If you would like to read more on this topic, there is a book entitled <u>Thanks</u> by Dr. Robert A. Emmons, published by Houghton Mifflin Company. In his book, Dr. Emmons quotes various studies that statistically confirm the benefits which result from developing an attitude of gratitude. The claims in his book are rather extraordinary. It is worth checking out.

An example of a "Thankful List Sheet"
can be found in the appendix

Faith Stone 15

Be Visionary

Nehemiah Chapter 1 tells the story of a visionary. Nehemiah was a Jewish man living under the rule of King Artaxerxes in the Persian government. He had been living in exile all of his life. He had never known anything but captivity. He began to hear that the Jews were starting to return to the Promised Land. They were returning to Jerusalem to rebuild the city, its walls, and its temple. But the news coming back from Jerusalem was not good. The province of Judah was in great trouble and disgrace. The walls of Jerusalem had been torn down and its gates no longer existed. Nehemiah wept when hearing the news. He wanted so much to be a part of the restoration of Israel.

Nehemiah got to work. For you see, Nehemiah was a visionary. If he ever had a chance to return to Israel, he would be prepared.

Upon hearing of the plight of Jerusalem, Nehemiah entered into a time of fasting, prayer, and repentance that lasted several months. Through his visioning, Nehemiah imagined the walls, the city, and the Temple. He worked and refined his plan. He had lists of what was needed to accomplish the task. He was ready to go. Nehemiah prayed the Lord would put in the King's heart great favor towards him and his plan. He also prayed for the right timing to approach the King. Then, on that divine day, the King asked Nehemiah why he looked so sad. Nehemiah took the opportunity and shared his heart about Jerusalem and his plan to rebuild the walls. The King responded by granting Nehemiah's wish to go to Jerusalem. However, Nehemiah did not stop the conversation there. Remember, Nehemiah was prepared. He immediately asked the King for everything he needed from his list to complete the task—the financial support of the King, to be granted the title of Governor of Judah, letters to governors granting him safe passage through hostile territory, letters granting him permission to get timber from the royal forest, the manpower and transportation needed to get to Jerusalem, etc.

When Nehemiah arrived in Jerusalem, he had a vision of what needed to be done, the necessary materials, the necessary funding, the authority to make decisions, and he had the Lord God Jehovah on his side. The end result was that the wall around Jerusalem was built in just 52 days. In the process, religious reforms and a spiritual awakening began. Nehemiah's ability to pray, plan, organize, and lead were crucial aspects of the project. Yet it was his passion and his ability to envision the completed project that led the way to the walls becoming a reality.

I believe we need to cultivate in youth an ability to be visionary in their thinking. Being visionary is acquiring the skill to be able to imagine and see things that are not yet present. These items may be physical in nature (Nehemiah's walls of Jerusalem) or they could be activity-oriented (like planning a church outing or a service project). Unfortunately, many youth do not have a person in their life that intentionally helps them nurture this type of thinking. Youth find themselves primarily dealing with what is right in front of them in the here and now. There are few opportunities for youth to engage in visionary thinking.

Visioning is something younger children do all the time when playing and pretending. Young children can quickly turn an empty refrigerator box into a spaceship, a pirate vessel, or a submarine. Give children a couple of old tires, some wood boards, and a couple of lawn chairs, and a sports car will emerge. As we get older, however, it seems that our busyness consumes our imagination time. Our thinking becomes more bound by limitations, and possibilities get pushed to the background.

I like to start the visioning process by taking youth outside to a familiar open field where they have had previous experiences. In our case, this can be done on our church property. Behind the church is a picnic shelter, next to an open field, and this makes the perfect place to begin our conversation.

So, there we stand one adult and a group of middle school students, staring at an empty field behind our church building. I ask the question, "What do you see?" I pause and wait for their responses. The first time we do this experience there can be a long stretch of silence. Silence is okay as we are letting the idea simmer awhile in their minds.

Eventually, students begin to say things like, "I see grass. I see a tree. I see dirt."

Then, I say, "Those are all true statements. Now this time, let's look deeper. What do you see?" I will continue in this line of questioning for several minutes to see if there's anyone in the group who has a natural tendency to envision an object or activity taking place that is not currently present.

If someone says, "I remember playing games in this field last summer," I then take his or her statement and ask more questions to help verbally paint the picture of what he or she sees in the field.

Often times, when I first do this experience with middle school students, I have to prompt them a bit further to get them thinking. I will say, "Last July, we held our Vacation Bible School games in this field. Do you remember?"

I immediately get responses such as, "Sure, I remember. I was there." "Yeah, we were out here every day." I then ask students to envision playing a game they played last summer in the field. That's when young people begin to see something in the field besides grass, trees, and dirt.

Someone will say "Yeah, we played kickball right over there."

And I will respond with, "Okay, do you remember where you stood in the field when it was the other team's turn to kick the ball? Do you remember who was pitching? Tell me who else was on your team. Paint the picture for me. Where was first base? Second base? Home plate?"

As this image emerges, I ask, "Okay, now can someone else tell me about something you've seen going on in this field that happened in the past?" As students share what they remember seeing in the field, I help them to repaint the picture with as much detail and clarity as possible.

To move students into a broader sense of visionary thinking, I introduce to them an idea that is initially beyond their imagination. I say, "Wouldn't it be super cool if the church had a swimming pool and we called it the St. John's Swim Club?" Students immediately love the idea. I ask them to look and then eventually walk out into the field and show me where the pool could be located. As I'm asking questions such as, "Where would the deep end be? Where would the shallow end be?" you can begin to see their wheels turning. "Where along the side would you put the water slide? Where is the diving board? Where are the lifeguard chairs?" Notice how I now change my questions to the present tense. The image really sharpens and becomes real when I ask students to close their eyes and hear the sounds of children laughing, water splashing, and lifeguards blowing their whistles.

At this point, students are catching on to the vision. When I ask the group if they see anything else, they start to tell me not only where the concession stand will be, but also where the shower house, picnic tables, and the umbrellas and chairs are located. They even pick out colors for the umbrellas and chairs!

What started out as a field of rocks and grass became a place of fun memories followed by an experience of visioning something that was not there yet, an amazing Swim Club that would draw families and community children to our church. Now, we do not actually have a pool in our church backyard, and we probably never will, but I bet you can imagine it being there. And most importantly, our young people can envision and image it there, too. I believe it is important for young people to be able to imagine and envision things that are not yet present.

I do this exercise with young people whenever I get the opportunity. It works especially well if I know something is going to be built somewhere around town. We head to that location, and I ask students what they see. Eventually, I share with them what the owner envisions and plans to build, making the point that everything that has ever been built, designed, or invented had to first be imagined in someone's mind. Our lives are better because of those who have envisioned something that was not yet there.

Youth, who utilize this visionary skill, can unpack a plethora of possibilities when planning projects. Being visionary in thinking can also help set a direction for the future. When I ask middle school students about their future plans, many mention an activity they hope to do in high school. Marching band is a common extra-curricular activity in our school district, so it is easy to ask questions to future band members. "What instrument do you see yourself playing? What does your uniform look like? Where do you practice your instrument? How does it feel to play your instrument well? How often do you practice? What does it look like for you to use your God-given talent on the field?

Off the field?" Asking such questions helps teens to visualize things not yet in existence.

The church needs people of vision. Spending time helping youth to develop this creative area of thinking is well worth it. Their ministry as adults will benefit greatly by the development of this Faith Stone.

Faith Stone 16

Spend Time with
People the Way Jesus Did

The Gospels are full of great stories where Jesus encounters people. These can be categorized into four different types of groupings. Jesus spent time with masses, the 72 (disciples), the 12 (apostles), and the 3 (Peter, James, and John).

I utilize these Bible stories to explain to youth that they should follow the example of Christ and spend time with believers in the same four ways. If Jesus felt it was important to spend time with masses, the 72, the 12, and the 3 then shouldn't we also do the same?

A good way to start this conversation with students is to read scripture passages where Jesus encounters these various groupings of people. This helps to define the masses, the 72, the 12, and the 3 in Jesus' life.

- The Masses: Jesus spent time with masses of people, many of whom were believers. (Matthew 14:13-21)

- The 72: Jesus had many disciples; however, he chose 72 to receive special training and sent them out to carry his message. (Luke 10:1-12)

- The 12: Jesus had twelve main companions who walked along side of him on the journey of life, with whom he spent most of his days, who were aware of the daily ups and downs of life, and with whom he found friendship. (Mark 3:13-19)

- The 3: On numerous occasions Jesus was in a very small group. During these times, he repeatedly took along with him the same three friends, Peter, James, and John. (Luke 9:28)

After we walk through biblical examples from each category, I ask youth to jot down when they spend time with believers in each of the four different areas. I also expand the definition of the four areas to include modern day examples.

The Masses: Youth need to be in the presence of hundreds, even thousands, of believers once or twice a year so they maintain the idea they are not alone in their Christian faith walk. There are millions of believers who have the same convictions and beliefs as they do. I encourage youth to attend events where there are masses of Christians. Music festivals, church-wide gatherings, and Christian service organizations are good examples where hundreds, sometimes thousands, of other believers gather together.

Experiences like this can be quite reassuring when youth are from smaller congregations and feel like they are the only ones at school or on their sports team who are living out their faith.

The 72: For many, "the 72" is their congregational worship service. Youth need to gather together weekly and be in the presence of others who are being equipped and then "sent out" into the world. Think of "the 72" as an extended family of faith, meeting the need for the relationship voids in our life. Within our congregation, we discover the treasure of spiritual grandmas and grandpas, moms and dads, aunts and uncles, brothers and sisters, cousins, nieces, and nephews. There is something important about having an extended spiritual family of 50 to 100 people in our lives. These people are role models for living out the faith and also sojourners with us in this broken world. Keeping that in mind, another place for youth to experience the 72 is to volunteer with a church-led community service project or to attend a church retreat that other youth groups will be attending. Regardless of the place, when youth spend time with other believers, they are renewed in faith and service.

The 12: *Who are "the 12" in your life? Who are the people of faith with whom you are close?* Asking youth to identify their 12 creates a sense of belonging and importance. In essence, they know "I belong and someone cares about me." They have friends with whom they can share, play, laugh, cry, serve, and pray together.

Having the opportunity to speak in scores of churches, I have noticed that many church youth groups seem to stall around the number 12. Sometimes a few more and sometimes a few less, but it seems like no matter what they do, they cannot grow their youth groups beyond that magical number of about 12. Sure, it is nice to have a large youth group, but it certainly is not the end of the world if you do not. It is reassuring to know that if Jesus had a group of 12 then we can too. Twelve is a good number of extended friends to have, to live life with, and to belong to. Because of this, I ask youth to specifically identify the people of faith with whom they are closest.

The 3: Then there are "the three," those with whom Jesus not only spent the most time, but with whom he spent his mountain top and valley experiences. The three were Peter, James, and John. It seems that wherever Jesus went, He was dragging along Peter, James, and John. And so, I ask students, "Who are your three? Who is in your inner circle; someone you spend more time with in deep conversation? Who do you turn to when you need someone to talk to? Who do you trust?" This is when I remind youth how important it is that their inner circle be people of faith and that they be involved in a church. Church is a good place to develop and nurture deeper relationships and to discover best friends, which is crucial to faith development.

In Mark 2:1-5 there is a story of true friendship. It is a story of a time when Jesus returned to Capernaum and was staying in a house. Word of His arrival quickly spread. Soon the house was packed with visitors anxious to hear what Jesus had to say. Not one more person could fit inside the house. Four men arrived carrying a paralyzed man on a mat. They could not get to Jesus through the crowd. Somehow the men got onto the roof of the house, made a hole in the roof, and then lowered their friend down to where Jesus was sitting. Whoa, now that's friendship!

I ask students, "Who are your close friends? Do you have people in your life that would do anything for you even at great sacrifice to themselves? Do you have friends who care enough about you to rip the roof right off a house in order to help you get to Jesus? Are you that friend?"

Greater love has no one than this: that he lay down his life for his friends. (John 15:13, NIV)

I believe it is important for youth to have contact with people of faith in all four of the areas listed above. I encourage students to think of ways they can engage with others like Jesus did. Spending time with people the way Jesus did is another good Faith Stone to have in your Faith Bag.

Imagine opening your bag and seeing the names, faces, and experiences of masses of people with whom you have spent time, as well as a group of people with whom you worship regularly. Imagine seeing in your bag healthy relationships with a dozen or so people of faith you know well, who are going the same direction as you. Imagine seeing in your bag a handful of best friends with whom to share your everyday experiences. How immeasurable that would be!

Faith Stone 17

Understand
the Five Love Languages

Our resource for helping youth understand love languages is a book written by Dr. Gary Chapman called The 5 Love Languages. We find it extremely valuable for youth to understand their primary love language, as well as the primary love language of those around them. Learning to speak another's love language does wonders for building strong, healthy, long-lasting relationships. Because relationships are of utmost importance, we believe it is a faith skill that youth need to have in their bag.

Visit www.5lovelanguages.com for more resources on love languages. Dr. Chapman has books designed specifically for men, women, teens, children, and coworkers. There is also an online quiz to help one determine his or her love language. It takes only a few minutes to complete and is an excellent tool for starting the conversation of love languages with students.

Dr. Chapman explains that the five love languages are *quality time, acts of service, physical touch, words of affirmation*, and *receiving gifts*. Just as we learn to speak a language (or dialects) to effectively communicate with others, we need to learn to speak each other's love languages for others to feel most loved. When we speak each other's love languages, we have learned how to best show appreciation and love to the people closest to us.

My wife's primary love language is *acts of service.* After a long day of going about her daily duties, my wife feels most loved if I unload the dishwasher, clean up the kitchen, or start the laundry. She much prefers these *acts of service* over being surprised with an occasional gift. The love language of *receiving gifts* scored the lowest when she took the quiz.

I have seen quite a few situations where spouses, parents, and children bettered their relationships by taking the love language quiz and then taking the results into consideration when expressing love and appreciation. They learn to appreciate those they love, and those closest to them feel loved. It's a win-win situation.

We are commanded in John 13:34 to love one another. How do we do that? Dr. Gary Chapman would tell you that we all have a love tank. And when this love tank is full, we can effectively go about our day. As Christians, we look for ways to fill each other's love tanks. Working with children and youth in the church, we begin to understand that the young person who is hanging around us might just be looking to fill their love tank with quality time. We start to realize why those who rank *physical touch* as their lowest love language might shy away from holding hands during prayer time. It also helps us understand which student needs that extra high five or comment of affirmation. Knowing love languages helps us as we work together to love children and youth into the Kingdom.

Her name is Mary, and she lives with her mom and dad. When Mary's mom came across the concept of Love Languages, she was curious to find out her daughter's top rated love language. Mary would soon be transitioning into her teenage years, and it was important to Mom that

Mary entered the turbulent teen years feeling totally loved and understood. When the online test results came back, Mom was not surprised at Mary's secondary love language, *quality time*. Mary would do anything to spend time together as a family, even if it meant routine trips to the grocery store. Mary cherished any time she was able to spend with Mom and Dad.

However, the discovery of Mary's primary love language was a bit unexpected. The love language ranked highest on her daughter's survey was *words of affirmation*. Now, Mom had always been good about affirming her daughter. She would put positive comments in her daughter's lunch bag, leave affirming notes when she left for work before Mary got up in the morning, and Mom made sure she complimented Mary on good behavior and school projects. Mary had always responded positively to these words of affirmation, but since she was getting older, Mom had begun to shy away from the note writing and compliments. Mom had wanted to respect her daughter's space and did not want to continue doing things that might make her feel like a child. As soon as Mom became aware that Mary's primary love language was *words of affirmation*, though, Mom asked Mary directly if she still wanted her to put care notes in Mary's lunch. Mary answered immediately with an enthusiastic, "Yes!" Mom resumed both the note writing and the conscious verbal affirmation of her daughter.

Looking to find a better way to connect, Mary's dad also decided to start leaving notes around the house for both Mom and Mary to find. As soon as Mary found the notes left for her, her face lit up. Mary quickly decided to return the favor. She began writing and placing care notes around the house for her father to find. A dad had become a hero just by leaving a few notes of affirmation around the house. Minimal effort, using the right love language, can create maximum results.

The story of Mary is both precious and priceless. If family members were simply aware of each other's love languages and then acted upon them, how much more improved our family relationships would be with each other. It is a simple concept that can easily be understood in half an hour, but the results are long lasting. I believe understanding the concept of Love Languages and then knowing and acting upon the knowledge is paramount to good parenting. I certainly know understanding the love language of the children and youth in our congregation has made me a more effective faith coach.

The Christian faith is built upon relationships. The Love Language concept is simple and easy to understand. As it can have a great impact on others, it is just common sense for us to learn about this tool. Please consider investigating the concept, understanding it, and then helping others discover its power. For any parent, or for anyone in ministry, this is a Faith Stone worth adding to your Faith Bag. I encourage you to check out Dr. Chapman's books and website.

Faith Stone 18

Understand Yourself and Others

———————— ⸮⸮ ————————

Personality Temperaments help explain the observable differences, as well as describe the natural tendencies of how people take in information, make decisions, plan their lives, and re-energize. It refers to those aspects of an individual's personality that are often regarded as innate rather than learned. Much work has been done in the field of Personality Typing by renowned clinical psychologist and author David Keirsey. According to Keirsey, there are four personality temperaments and four variants of each temperament for a total of sixteen different personality types.

It is best to have a trained person run a personality temperament session. Yes, it is possible to start youth on the process of understanding the basic concept of personality temperaments; however, it is suggested that a trained person be present whenever there is a desire to go deeper than the basics. If not presented well, the session can quickly turn into a time of laughing and teasing as students focus on their differences. Feelings can easily get hurt as youth label and categorize each other. If used incorrectly, it can be a damaging experience for both individual young people and group dynamics. If used appropriately, an understanding of the personality temperament is a wonderful tool that can be utilized for faith development in youth.

I found having an understanding of the concept of temperaments so vital to my work with young people that I went on to acquire a personality temperament certification through Keirsey.com. It is the most powerful instrument I have come across for helping young people figure out how the Lord God Almighty has created them, and with that knowledge they can better discover how they fit into this world.

In our congregation, we introduce youth to the temperament concept in middle school. Using material from Keirsey, we walk students through simple exercises to help them discover which of the four personality temperaments they best identify with. During this session, we can help youth understand whether they are concrete or abstract thinkers, and we can help them to discover if they are cooperative or utilitarian in their actions. We also talk with students about the characteristics of each of the four temperaments. Just acquiring this information alone is a positive step forward in self-awareness.

In this first session, our aim is not to pigeonhole youth into a temperament, but simply for students to learn that some of us are wired differently than others. The main point is for youth to grasp the concept that they are not weird and those around them are not weird, but that we are all uniquely wired by God. The point is made that we need all four temperaments present for our faith community to function best.

After this first session, there always seem to be some students who take a special interest in the topic of temperaments. With these students, we give them the opportunity to take the youth version of the temperament sorter. The sorter is a questionnaire of seventy questions. As a result of taking the sorter, students receive detailed reports about their particular temperament and how this relates to them on subjects such as career interests, learning styles, and leadership and management tendencies.

Once students have a general understanding of their personality temperament, we are better able to help them to grow in their faith, to discover their gifts, to interact with people, to be stronger leaders and managers, and to become involved in meaningful ministry tailored specially to their temperament.

Having basic knowledge of the personality temperament also helps us to better understand why some youth always stay between the behavior lines while others always seem to be stepping over the lines. It helps to explain why people have differing opinions and reactions to common church practices; for example, why parishioners prefer certain but differing styles of worship or why some people like to pray quietly by themselves while others prefer to pray out loud in groups. It also gives perspective and understanding as to why some people want the "passing of the peace" to go on for 20 minutes, while others have an immediate heighted sense of anxiety at the mere thought of having to interact with anyone in such a personal way during a worship service.

Greg was a quiet young man who, although confident in his abilities, pretty much kept to himself. He took the Keirsey temperament analysis sorter when he was a freshman in college. His score resulted in his temperament being identified as an INTJ (Mastermind). A brief explanation of the role variant was included with the test results. The summary indicated his temperament was rare, comprising of less than 1% of the population. The summary went on to say that INTJs are private people. They are rarely seen in social situations or they tend to avoid them. INTJs are capable leaders

| **Introverted (I) or Extroverted (E)** |
| **Sensory (S) or Intuitive (N)** |
| **Feeling (F) or Thinking (T)** |
| **Judging (J) or Perceiving (P)** |

who prefer to stay in the background, can become single-minded at times, and value efficiency above all else. The emotions of an INTJ are hard to read, which often results in acquaintances and coworkers having a difficult time getting to know them. They often come across as emotionally distant, when, in fact, they are focusing on the task at hand, constantly analyzing ways to improve whatever situation in which they find themselves. INTJs are the ultimate planners, always having backup plans in place. They have an eye for long term strategic planning and are an asset to whatever organization with which they are associated.

Whoa, the summary nailed Greg. It explained his desire to avoid social situations, the emotional distance he often felt with people, and his tendencies to have just a few carefully chosen close friends. The description of his propensity for analyzing situations and his tendency toward long-term thinking explained much. Learning that less than 1% of the population functioned the way he did was helpful to know. Understanding that his virtues would someday be valued as necessary assets to an organization reassured Greg that he was a worthwhile person with something to offer. Just knowing someone with professional credentials understood him and that he was acknowledged as being "normal" was extremely comforting.

Greg discovered that he was not painfully different. He had been hard-wired by God himself, created specifically for good works. This simple basic understanding of himself changed his entire view of who he was and what he was capable of becoming. What great knowledge to have! This basic understanding makes it much easier for youth to find their place in this world.

Then there was Laura. By taking the sorter she discovered she was an ESFP (Performer). One of the attributes of this type is the extrovert (E). Laura, as an extrovert, was re-energized by spending time with people and, from her perspective, the more people the better. After spending time with lots of people, Greg often found himself emotionally drained, needing to withdraw from people in order to re-energize. While Greg gravitated towards being by himself or with a small number of people, Laura would rather be with lots of people performing, sharing, and enjoying the interaction. To Laura, the entire world was a stage.

While Greg was logically thinking through goals and objectives (T), Laura was walking a mile in the shoes of others (F). While Greg was making decisions and sticking to them (J), Laura was taking advantage of the moment and postponing the making of decisions until absolutely necessary (P).

Greg and Laura have two completely opposite temperaments; yet, both have been created by God as they are and each possesses special talents. Yes, they are wired differently, yet each possesses important attributes. We are all especially blessed when each personality temperament is represented within the faith community.

Much like the concept of Love Languages, the self-awareness that comes from understanding the basics of personality temperament theory is a Faith Stone worth adding to your Faith Bag.

Connect with Gary if you are interested
in having your group experience a
personality temperament training session

125

Faith Stone 19

Develop a Biblical Self-Esteem

The shopping mall and retail stores are losers. Or maybe it would be better worded that retail stores send the message, "You are a loser." Do you and I go to retails stores and the mall? Yep, but it still makes most of us feel like losers. As you walk down the middle of the mall, every shop window screams out at you that unless you own "this" or wear "that," you don't measure up. Clothing, electronic gadgets, exercise equipment, tempting foods, and kiosks set our standards on what is valued. Our children are growing up surrounded by messages that constantly tell them they cannot be whole, happy, and popular unless they acquire the newest and best thing on the market.

Added to this pressure to acquire is the pressure to be something that is unattainable. Our world values air-brushed beauty that can only be seen on billboards or magazine covers and massive muscles that can't be acquired except with drugs. It is no wonder our youth can't measure up to the world's standards of success and beauty and, as a result, quickly feel inadequate.

So, how do we raise godly young men and women who know the truth about their value and self-worth? We focus on who God says we are. I believe our self-esteem should be based on the Word of God. Thus, our aim is to build a Biblical self-esteem in the youth of our congregation by developing in them a spiritual foundation based on God's word.

A favorite Bible story of mine comes from Judges, chapter 6. In this chapter, Gideon was a young man who finds himself threshing wheat in a winepress pit. During this time period, the Israelites were victims of the Midianites who came each harvest and stole everything the Israelites had worked so hard to plant and cultivate. As Gideon was performing his duty, "the angel of the Lord appeared to Gideon and said, 'Mighty hero, the Lord is with you!'" (Judges 6:12, NLT)

How interesting the angel of the Lord addressed Gideon in this fashion. Gideon was a young man at the time, full of doubts, fears, and feelings of inadequacy. I am sure Gideon did not venture himself to be a "mighty hero!" Yet God knew who Gideon would become. And yes, Gideon went on to be a "mighty hero" in the kingdom of God by rescuing the nation of Israel from the hand of the Midianites.

As I begin the discussion about biblical self-esteem with young people, I tell the story of Gideon's encounter with the angel. I tell students that although Gideon had no idea he was going to become a mighty hero, God did, and He treated Gideon as such right then! I go on to tell students that although I had no idea decades ago what I would be doing for God today, if an angel of the Lord appeared to me when I was a young man, he may have addressed me as, "Oh Gary, GREAT and MIGHTY youth director..."

I then ask youth, "If an angel of the Lord appeared to you today, how would the angel address you?" I give them some examples based on their strengths. *Oh Steve, GREAT and MIGHTY guitar player. Oh Kim, GREAT and MIGHTY VBS leader. Oh Cheryl, GREAT and MIGHTY song leader. Oh Scott, GREAT and MIGHTY service project coordinator.* I say these statements even though students are not yet proficient in their skills. I take the whole concept a step further and treat them as though they have already become what they may be in the future. This idea raises the bar on standards and behavior. I tend to find that young people strive to live up to these expectations as they are searching for an identity.

One tool we use that helps our teens to start building a biblical self-esteem is the "I AM" sheet. The "I AM" sheet is a list of Bible verses that describes who we are in the sight of God. We give students a copy of the following list and then throughout the coming years, we highlight different verses, at different times, and in different ways. We are hoping youth will commit some of these verses to memory so that when they encounter a world that challenges their self-worth, they can respond by quoting scripture. (See Matthew 4:4, 4:7, and 4:10.)

If you read the verses below, you can see how powerful it can be to change the verses into living truths.

I AM...

1. Obeying the Lord's commandments (Deuteronomy 28:13)
2. Blessed wherever I go (Deuteronomy 28:6)
3. Holy for thou art Holy (Leviticus 19:2)
4. Redeemed from the hand of the enemy (Psalm 107:2)
5. The salt of the earth (Matthew 5:13)
6. The light of the world (Matthew 5:14)
7. Establishing God's Word here on earth (Matthew 16:19)
8. Exercising my authority over the enemy (Luke 10:19)
9. A child of God (John 1:12)

10. Part of the true vine, and Christ's life flows through me (John 15:1, 5)
11. Chosen by Christ to bear fruit (John 15:16)
12. Christ's witness sent out to tell everybody about Him (Acts 1:8)
13. Justified (Romans 5:1)
14. A slave of righteousness (Romans 6:18)
15. A slave to God, making me holy and giving me eternal life (Romans 6:22)
16. Free from the punishment my sins deserve (Romans 8:1)
17. Led by the Spirit of God (Romans 8:14)
18. An heir of God and a joint heir with Jesus Christ (Romans 8:17)
19. More than a conqueror (Romans 8:37)
20. Being transformed by a renewed mind (Romans 12:1-2)
21. Given the mind of Christ. He gives me His wisdom to make right decisions (I Corinthians 2:16)
22. Working as partners with those who belong to God (I Corinthians 3:9)
23. Sanctified (I Corinthians 6:11)
24. Joined forever to the Lord and am one spirit with Him (I Corinthians 6:17)
25. A temple of the Holy Spirit who lives in me (I Corinthians 6:19)
26. Bought with a price, I am not my own, I belong to God (I Corinthians 6:19-20)
27. God's possession, chosen and secure in Him. I have been given the Holy Spirit as a promise of my inheritance to come (II Corinthians 1:21-22)
28. No longer living for myself, but for Christ (II Corinthians 5:14-15)
29. A part of Christ's body (I Corinthians 12:27)
30. Not troubled by what I see (II Corinthians 4:18)

31. Walking by faith and not by sight (II Corinthians 5:7)
32. A new creature (II Corinthians 5:17)
33. At peace with God and He has given me the work of helping others find peace with Him (II Corinthians 5:18-19)
34. The righteousness of God in Christ (II Corinthians 5:21)
35. Bringing every thought into captivity (II Corinthians 10:5)
36. Redeemed from the curse of the law (Galatians 3:13)
37. A child of God and one with others in His family (Galatians 3: 26, 28)
38. A child of God who will receive the inheritance that He has promised (Galatians 4:6-7)
39. A saint, a holy person (Ephesians 1:1)
40. Blessed with all spiritual blessings (Ephesians 1:3)
41. A citizen of heaven (Ephesians 2:6)
42. Saved by grace through faith (Ephesians 2:8-9)
43. God's building project, His handiwork, created in Christ to do His work (Ephesians 2:10)
44. Able to have direct access to the Father through the Spirit (Ephesians 2:18)
45. A member of God's household (Ephesians 2:19)
46. A prisoner of Christ so that I may help others (Ephesians 3:1)
47. Able to approach God with freedom and confidence (Ephesians 3:12)
48. Righteous and holy (Ephesians 4:24)
49. Following the example of Christ (Ephesians 5:1)
50. Strong in the Lord and the power of His might (Ephesians 6:10)
51. Conducting myself in a manner worthy of the Gospel (Philippians 1:27)

52. Doing all things through Christ who strengthens me (Philippians 4:13)
53. Getting all of my needs met by Jesus (Philippians 4:19)
54. Delivered from the powers of darkness (Colossians 1:13)
55. Forgiven (Colossians 1:14)
56. Firmly rooted in Christ and overflowing with thankfulness (Colossians 2:7)
57. Complete in Christ (Colossians 2:10)
58. Spiritually clean. My old sinful self has been removed (Colossians 2:11)
59. Chosen of God, holy and dearly loved (Colossians 3:12)
60. A child of light and not of darkness (I Thessalonians 5:5)
61. Chosen to share in God's heavenly calling (Hebrews 3:1)
62. One of God's living stones, being built up in Christ as a spiritual house (I Peter 2:5)
63. A member of a chosen race, a royal priesthood, a holy nation, a people belonging to God (I Peter 2:9-10)
64. Only a visitor to this world in which I temporarily live (I Peter 2:11)
65. Healed by His wounds (I Peter 2:24)
66. An enemy of evil (I Peter 5:8)
67. A partaker of His divine nature (II Peter 1:4)
68. Daily overcoming the devil (I John 4:4)
69. An inheritor of eternal life (I John 5:11-12)
70. Born of God and the evil one cannot touch me (I John 5:18)
71. An overcomer by the blood of the Lamb (Revelations 12:11)

It is important to revisit these verses often. Sometimes, we highlight a verse and then connect with the verse for several meetings in a row. Sometimes, youth will meet in small groups and take a verse and create a skit to perform for the larger group. Sometimes, we will do a craft with a verse of their choice that students can then display in a place where they will see it every day. Occasionally, we have youth create bookmarks using one of the verses to be used either in their Bibles or at school. Regardless of the approach, we come back and revisit the "I AM" verses over and over again. We are convinced that if you have a true understanding of what scripture says about you, you will walk confident and tall in the midst of a world full of turmoil.

Imagine young people going through their day believing they are children of God, they are blessed wherever they go, they are a royal priesthood, they are not troubled by what they see, they are joint heirs with Jesus Christ, they are no longer living for themselves but for Christ, and they have been given the mind of Christ so as to make good decisions. Wow, I am telling you, a person who is constantly reminded by the Holy Spirit of such truths is going to win most of the spiritual battles that come his or her way.

When David stood before Goliath, he knew he was God's chosen and that the battle belonged to the Lord. This truth gave him the confidence to stand before his enemies and to be victorious. Knowing who you are and *whose* you are is definitely a Faith Stone we want students to have in their Faith Bags.

Faith Stone 20

Be Able to Introduce Yourself

————⌒⌁⌒————

First impressions are lasting impressions.

W hen Mallory was a freshman in college, she contacted me and thanked me for teaching her the technique of an introduction. During her first few days in college,
Mallory found herself in an entry level communications
course. Early on in the course, the professor had each student do an introductory speech. One by one, students stood
up and hemmed and hawed their way through the basics of
saying their name, where they were from, their major, etc.
Mallory said it was painful to watch as most students strug-
gled their way through the exercise.

When it was Mallory's turn, she simply stood up, smiled,
and said,

> "In 1983, I almost didn't make it into this world.
> However, prayers started before my birth sustained
> me then and ever since, making faith the center of
> who I am today.
>
>   I am from Grove City, Ohio. My name is Mallory.
> I was born and raised in Grove City and attended
> Grove City High School where I spent four years

in the marching band, with the last two years in the flag corp. I also attended St. John's Lutheran Church where I spent much of my time as a teen.

I am excited about being here at the university where I will be studying early childhood development. What I hope to gain from Professor Smith's Communications course is a greater ability to express my ideas in both written and verbal form to both children and adults."

Whoa, there was silence in the room as Mallory sat down. She had nailed the introduction. In less than 30 seconds, Mallory had earned the respect of everyone in the room, including her professor. She was equipped, prepared, and she had confidently delivered.

As Mallory shared her story with me, I was not surprised. We taught her how to introduce herself four years earlier when she was a freshman in high school. Then, over the next four years, Mallory found herself in many situations where she needed to introduce herself. By the time she was a freshman in college, Mallory had introduced herself scores of times. It had become second nature to her.

While this may not at first be viewed as a "faith" skill, we have found it to be a worthwhile one for youth to know and to have practiced. Over the course of their lives, students will constantly find themselves in situations where they need to introduce themselves. Imagine a student's confidence as he or she reaches into a trusted bag of skills ready to be used at a moment's notice. First impressions are lasting impressions. It is our aim to give youth the benefit of a positive impression that will help them in their personal ministry.

This skill is best learned in a group. We start by handing out a sheet of paper to students, asking them to fill in the blanks...

- What is your name?
- Where were you born?
- Where do you go to school (or work)?
- What is an interesting fact about yourself or something you like to do?
- What is one thing you'd like to gain from this experience (whatever the group is going to be doing)?

After students have had a few minutes to write down their answers, we stand in front of the group and give two or three examples of what an introductory talk would look like. After hearing several sample introductions, or better yet, several prepared leaders introducing themselves, we then give each student the opportunity to introduce him or herself to the group.

At this point, we're not looking for perfect introductions. The goal is affirmation. After a student introduces himself, we lead the group in applauding the student for getting in front of the group and for practicing this newly acquired skill. A student's soul should sweetly reverberate and swell with the clapping and cheers.

Practice, encouragement, and affirmation are foundational to building skills in students. Keeping this in mind, let's go to our next faith skill: "Story Talk Training." The introductory talk and faith talks actually work well together as we strive to equip students in sharing their faith.

> An example of the "Introductory Story Talk" sheet can be found in the appendix

Faith Stone 21

Develop Faith-Based
Story Talk Skills

One of the skills we want to impart to our young people is how to give faith talks. A faith talk is simply a talk given to a group of people for the purpose of sharing, affirming, and encouraging others in the faith.

I was blessed to have been trained to speak to groups by a man who is considered to be a master trainer. He spent his career training company executives on how to speak in front of people. During his retirement years, he developed a leadership and management course for those going into youth ministry. I attended the training multiple times and eventually became part of his training team.

Youth Ministry was the focal point of my career. Consequently, I took all of the great training I received and designed ways to make it workable for teens. One of the programs we developed is called "Story Talk training." The concept is simple. Jesus often taught by using stories. These stories were of everyday situations that were familiar to the crowds who were following Jesus. As a result, Jesus made connections with people and His stories were remembered.

Occasionally, I ask young people if they remember anything from a recent sermon or from my talk from last week.

Often there's a pause of silence and then eventually someone will remember something he or she heard, and just about on every occasion what the person remembers is a story that was told. Because we tend to remember stories, the idea of basing faith talks on stories seemed the reasonable way to go.

Not only do stories help us to remember a teaching point, they connect us. Storyteller and author Donald Davis says, "A story is like a line, a wire between the teller and the listener. Both people hold each end of it, and the story walks on that wire between them." Stories link us together. In this connection, we are inspired, moved, grounded, and influenced.

Everyone loves a good story. Our students have stories to tell. They tell stories to each other all the time (in the lunch room, on the school bus, when hanging out together). What we do is help youth take a story they have already told and ease them into sharing it in front of a group of people. The older we get, the more stories we have to share. It is in these everyday stories that we talk about God, and faith, and life. As there are many different stories, there could be as many different story talks. But for the purpose of training youth in sharing their faith, we have come up with seven different story talks.

1. How to Introduce Yourself Story Talk
2. A Childhood Story Talk
3. A Lesson I Learned Story Talk
4. A Favorite Bible (Story, Verse, or Character) Story Talk
5. A Person in my Faith Web Story Talk
6. A God Sighting Story Talk
7. A Perseverance Story Talk

The system we have developed to teach faith talks has made it easy and natural for teens to learn how to speak in front of groups. We know that young people have hundreds of stories to share. They spend much of their free time with friends talking about what they did last night or this morning. Every time they attend a church service project or church trip, they come home with stories. What we do is have youth put some structure to the stories they are already sharing and then teach them how to add a faith point to their story. Finally, we ease them into doing so in front of a group.

Often, we start by having students sit at a table, make a list of stories, and then choose one to tell their friends. Next, while standing at their table, students can practice telling their story to three or four friends. Eventually, they tell their story in front of the entire group.

Affirmation and encouragement are very important throughout this process, but especially when a student is giving a talk in front of a group. Practice, affirmation, and a good experience all lend themselves to building confidence in a student. We always focus on the positive. When a student does something exceptionally well, we point that out to other students. To not embarrass a shy student, I will even ask if I may make a teaching point to the group on something note-worthy about the student's talk. Keeping the positive in the forefront sets the bar for other students to achieve.

Once prepared, we ease students into situations by giving them the opportunity to speak to preschoolers or elementary school age children. As students gain confidence, they eventually use a microphone and end up in front of a larger and/ or older audience.

After 30 years of training young people, we know that if a youth has the desire, the willingness to learn, and is coach-able, we can train him or her to give a quality faith talk. This is a golden skill, and confidence soars when they are able and prepared to speak in front of a group. What a great Faith Stone to add to the Faith Bag!

Interested in hearing more about
Story Talk Training? Contact Gary through
www.faithwebbing.com

Faith Stone 22

Find Your Million Dollar Mate

There are a variety of good materials on the market that help church leaders to discuss the topic of dating and marriage with teens. A resource we use is a book called <u>Finding Your Million Dollar Mate</u> by Randy Pope. The author presents a profoundly simple and easy to understand set of guidelines towards finding your million dollar mate. After reading the book, you can take the author's concept, and in about ten minutes, you can explain to teenagers not only how to find your million dollar mate, but how to have a growing marriage that will last a lifetime. It has been a great resource for us. To fully understand his concepts, consider purchasing Randy Pope's book or check it out from your local library. It is inexpensive and a short read.

We do a couple of exercises with youth to help prepare them for their million dollar mate. The first thing we do is encourage youth to pray for their potential future spouse every day. Remember the everyday prayer sheet? We make sure students add their potential spouse to the sheet. A student could then write out a prayer that looks something like this:

Dear Lord, I pray for my potential spouse today that you would keep him/her safe, healthy, and actively growing in his/her faith. Prepare me for him/her and prepare him/her for me. Amen.

Another exercise we do with students is have them jot down on a piece of paper all of the qualities they are looking for in a spouse. Youth usually really get into this exercise. It is not uncommon for the lists to get lengthy. Like, unrealistically long! It is fun to have students share their lists with each other. As they share the qualities they are looking for in a spouse, I think, "Even Jesus wouldn't make the cut."

After students share and the giggles in the room have subsided, I tell the young men in the room, "If you want to marry a princess, then you have to become a prince."

And to the young ladies in the room, I say, "If you want to marry a prince, then you have to become a princess."

Yep, the qualities they were looking for in a spouse just became a list of qualities they need to build into themselves. Their list has become a yardstick from which to measure who they are and who they are becoming.

Next, I ask students to rank themselves on each quality on a scale from 1 to 5 (one being the lowest score and 5 being the highest score). If possible, I collect the sheets, copy them, and return the original. Once I have a copy of their rankings, it gives me a natural future avenue with which to remind students of their own goals. For example, if a student is ever harsh with someone, I can kindly remind him or her that a quality he or she was hoping to grow was gentleness. This conversation is done sensitively and privately. Throughout the years, it is helpful to revisit the quality lists with students and have them rescore themselves to see where they are growing and maturing in character.

When Abby was in seventh grade, she was in Sunday school the day I suggested they begin praying daily for their future spouse. Abby's first thoughts were, "Well, I don't have to do this because I'm not planning on getting married." But, upon further thought, she decided, "Maybe I better start praying for my spouse anyway....just in case." So, in seventh grade, Abby began praying every day for her future spouse...just in case. Years later, when Abby was in her middle 20s, I heard she became engaged. Soon after, she contacted me and wanted to go out for dinner.

So, Abby and I went to a local restaurant where she proceeded to tell me the story of her fiancé and how she had prayed for him. She started by saying to me, "I want you to tell this story to as many people as you can."

She began to tell me what was running through her mind the day I first told her she should start praying for her spouse. She also told me how she continued to pray for her spouse often through middle school, high school, and beyond.

Years later, she eventually met the man of her dreams and became engaged. During their courtship, Abby discovered that when she was in seventh grade, her future husband had not yet become a person of faith. She told me the same year she began praying for her potential spouse was the same year her future husband came to the saving knowledge of Jesus Christ. Abby went on to tell me that praying daily for her future spouse was one of the best things she had ever done in her life.

She encouraged me to continue to tell young people to pray for their spouse every day and then reiterated, "You should tell this story to as many people as possible."

Do good things come from devoted, consistent prayer? Ask Abby. *Is it worth spending time every day praying for your future potential spouse?* Ask Abby. *Is it worth having the spiritual discipline of regular prayer in your Faith Bag?* Ask Abby, her devoted husband, and her dearly loved children!

Faith Stones 23–30

Faith Foundation Skills

A s spiritual disciplines are being developed in young people, and as personal understanding and people skills are being honed, we also strive to widen students' faith foundations by helping them attain basic faith skills.

We believe these faith foundation skills should be pursued by every one of us. At some point in our lives, we will likely be asked to open or close a meeting in prayer, lead a table grace, give a devotional before a meeting, or facilitate a basic Bible study.

We have both discovered and developed what we believe are methods that ease young people into acquiring such ministry Faith Stones. As David was prepared and ready, let's also be prepared.

Faith Stone 23

Know the Stories of God's People

H aving a working knowledge of the Word of God is of paramount importance. Jesus quoted scripture throughout the Gospels. When a Pharisee asked Jesus a question about the Law of Moses, Jesus replied with, *"Love the Lord your God with all your heart and with all your soul and with all your mind. This is the first and greatest commandment. And the second is like it: Love your neighbor as yourself. All the Law and the Prophets hang on these two commandments."* (Matthew 22:36-40, NLT)

Even when tempted by the evil one with the nations of the world and all their glory, Jesus responded by quoting Scripture. Jesus answered, "For the Scriptures say, 'You must worship the Lord your God; serve only him.'" (Matthew 4:10, NLT)

In Ephesians chapter 6, we are instructed to put on and wear the full armor of God. Of the six parts of the armor of God, five are defensive in nature. They protect us, helping us to stand our ground.

"Therefore put on the full armor of God, so that when the day of evil comes, you may be able to stand your ground, and after you have done everything, to stand." (Ephesians 6:13, NIV)

Only one piece of the armor of God is an offensive weapon. We see in verse 17 that it is "the Sword of the Spirit, which is the word of God." A sword is designed to attack an enemy. Not knowing the Word of God is like a soldier being in a war without a weapon.

I ask teenagers regularly, "What is better than learning from your mistakes?"

They know the answer, which is, "Learning from someone else's mistakes."

I tell youth we study the Word of God to learn from *the mistakes* of others. Likewise, we study the Word of God so we can also learn from *the successes* of others.

In our congregation, we have identified approximately 30 Old and 30 New Testament stories on which to build the foundation of our faith. We offer this two year study during middle school. Each Bible story has one main point that we address using various learning styles. Storytelling, a hands-on activity, video/music, and small group discussions are helpful tools to making the bible point.

We spend a year on each testament. The purpose of the teachings is to give the students a foundational framework of the Word of God. We subdivide each Testament into several headings, making it seem less daunting.

The five sections of the Old Testament are listed below. With each section, the students know a hand motion which reflects the theme of the books, as well as helps them to remember the order of the stories.

1. The Creation: Genesis
2. The Exodus: Exodus, Leviticus, Numbers, Deuteronomy
3. The Time of the Judges: Joshua, Judges, Ruth
4. The Time of the Kings: I & II Samuel, I & II Kings, I & II Chronicles, Psalms, Proverbs, Ecclesiastes, Song of Solomon

5. The Time of the Prophets: All the rest of the Old
   Testament books

We divide the New Testament into six sections, again with
hand motions that go with each section.

1. Jesus' Birth
2. Jesus' Teachings
3. Jesus' Death & Resurrection
4. The Book of Acts
5. The Letters
6. Celebration

I encourage congregations to offer students, at some point
in their educational system, a chance to go through the major
stories of the Bible in chronological order. Weekly topical
Bible studies are important; however, having a chronological framework of the Word of God helps youth to fit topical
studies within the entirety of the Bible. The Word of God
is complex. Once a framework of Biblical understanding is
acquired, the concepts of law, promises, genealogies, patri-
archs, judges, kings, prophets, grace, parables, and a call to
holy living make more sense and can be understood in right
relationship with each other.

Having a strong biblical foundation and an understanding
of the basic framework of the Word of God is a Faith Stone
that will reap huge benefits for young people throughout
their entire lives.

> ## Looking for a Bible Story speaker?
> ## Connect with Gary

Faith Stone 24

Know Your Bible and Its Study Tools

————————— ✺ —————————

I am a tennis player. My father was a high school tennis coach and taught tennis lessons in the community. I grew up around tennis. I had a tennis racket in my hand as soon as I was able to walk. When tennis players are younger, they all have that important decision to make, "Do I use a child's racket and at various points switch to larger size rackets until I am big enough to use the adult-sized racket? Or do I just start with the adult-sized racket and grow into it?" It's a tough decision with advantages and disadvantages to both options.

We had the same dilemma with youth and Bibles. There are tiny tot Bibles, children's Bibles, tween Bibles, middle school Bibles, youth Bibles, and adult study Bibles. There are a myriad of options. It's a tough choice because each option has its own advantages and disadvantages. As for now, this is where our church stands on the Bible dilemma. We use Bibles designed for younger students up through sixth grade. Then we skip the teen Bibles and give each middle school student an adult study Bible. It's been an excellent faith formation step in our congregation.

Beginning in seventh grade, all of our students receive the "great big" Bible. It's thick, about two inches thick, and heavy. But what we love about the adult study Bible is that it can be used for the rest of their lives. We have chosen the Life Application Study Bible. It comes in various translations. From seventh grade on, all of us are using the same Bible. Since our teens and adults are together so often, it has been wonderful for all of us to literally be on the same page.

The Life Application Study Bible has footnotes, cross references, a concordance, character profiles, maps, charts, measurement conversions, and timelines. It also has a couple of pages at the beginning of each book which provides the setting, author, audience, main characters, main points, an outline of the book, and more.

During a student's teen years, we introduce every tool available from the Life Application Study Bible. We want students to be equipped to find anything they are looking for in the Word of God. We also encourage youth to underline, highlight, and take notes directly in the margins of their Bible. We hope by the time students graduate from high school, their Bibles are well used, well-worn, and considered to be a treasured and necessary asset to their faith development. We hope that when they are asked the burning question, "If your house was on fire and you only had time to take one possession with you, what would you take?" the answer would be, "I would grab my Bible."

Faith Stone 25

Facilitate a Bible Study

A faith skill every believer should possess is the ability to facilitate a Bible study. Being the facilitator does not mean you have all of the answers, but that you help ensure everyone gets the opportunity to participate. The facilitator creates a positive environment where participants feel safe in sharing and exploring scripture. Yes, it is advantageous and desirable to attend a Bible study led by a trained theologian. However, most people I know often find themselves in Bible studies led by college students, camp counselors, Sunday school teachers, and/or congregational members. Some studies are led by the pastor, but many are not. Thus, we want to prepare our students to be able to facilitate a Bible study as the need arises.

Using the SOAP format (Faith Stone 4) keeps it simple. This study format is broken down into five key elements: prayer, study, observations, applications, and more prayer. Students can volunteer to lead the different areas. One student is the *facilitator*. He or she makes sure that students are assigned to these roles:

- *Time Keeper* keeps track of the time. He or she sets the time for coming back after individual study and watches the time to make sure the group study starts on time.
- *Prayer Person One* opens the group sharing with prayer.
- *Prayer Person Two* ends the sharing time by starting the closing prayer.
- *Prayer Person Three* ends the closing prayer after everyone in the group has had the opportunity to pray out loud or silently.

Each role of the study is fairly easy to do. All the *facilitator* does is to make sure the roles are done by different students in the group. Then the *facilitator* simply walks the group through the various sections of the Bible study format. The idea is to move the group along, asking students what they think or what they wrote down under a specific heading.

We believe, as leaders, we need to create an atmosphere where teens feel comfortable participating in the various roles of the small group study. We want students to rotate through the roles until all aspects of participating in a Bible study become second nature to them. Undoubtedly, in such a study, questions will arise that no one in the group will be able to answer. At this point, we encourage the group to revisit the question in subsequent weeks or, if the question proves too perplexing, to bounce it off of some older wiser adults (including the pastor).

Although relatively simple, many people shy away from leading a group discussion. We think facilitating a group gets easier with practice. So, we regularly provide opportunities for teens to take turns leading small group discussions. These discussions are often a few simple questions posed in Sunday school, at youth group sessions, on advances and retreats, or on summer church trips. Every chance we get, we put youth in groups of three to five and have students take turns facilitating a discussion. Over time, most become comfortable with facilitating the simple discussions. It then becomes an easy transition to facilitate a small faith growth group such as a Bible study.

This is a major skill to develop in young people. Just the concept alone of learning how to facilitate a group is worth knowing. From this one skill, youth learn how to ask good questions, actively listen, cushion responses, involve everyone in a discussion, and freely admit not knowing all of the answers. This Faith Stone is a big confidence builder.

Faith Stone 26

Lead Devotions

————⟨◌⟩————

It is nine o'clock on a warm summer evening in late June. Alyssa is about to lead devotions to a cabin of six elementary school age girls during the first night at camp. She is a bit nervous, but she is prepared. Alyssa knows the girls in her cabin from the weekly church club night. The girls also know and admire Alyssa and are ready to listen intently to what she has to say. She begins by telling a story of when she was scared to go on a ride at an amusement park. She asks the girls if they have ever been scared to go on an amusement park ride. She encourages them to tell their story. The girls laugh and giggle as they share their experiences. Alyssa then turns to her Bible and tells the girls the story of Peter walking on the water. She talks about how scared Peter must have been when he started to sink in the middle of the stormy lake. She talks about how when following Jesus the disciples probably often thought as if they were at an amusement park. There were lots of exciting times, but some scary times too. Alyssa ends by telling the girls that Jesus told the disciples throughout scripture to "fear not." In fact, Alyssa tells them the term "fear not" appears in the Bible over 300 times. So, whatever happens over the weekend camp experience, the girls should "fear not" because Jesus is with them.

Alyssa asks them to bow their heads and they end in a time of prayer.

The previous month Alyssa attended a session on leading devotions. Alyssa is a high school student who attended the session because she had been asked to lead the Friday night devotions at an upcoming elementary camp. Alyssa loves those little girls and the girls love Alyssa. She is the perfect person to give a faith ending to the day. She was ready. She was prepared.

This is another good Faith Stone for students to have in their Faith Bags; the ability to create and lead devotions. For the rest of their lives, they will have the opportunity to lead devotions. It might be as a youth or an adult. It may be to open a youth group meeting, a small group gathering, or a church council meeting. There are numerous situations where being able to lead a devotion is a skill worth having.

> An example of a worksheet to help youth develop a devotional can be found in the appendix

Faith Stone 27

Open/Close a Meeting in Prayer

A s with most of the skills we pass on to young people, we believe opening and closing a meeting in prayer is something every believer ought to be able to do. We have developed a method for students to acquire this skill. As with many of the skills mentioned in this book, we tend to start introducing the Faith Stones to youth somewhere between fifth and seventh grade. However, this particular skill can be introduced with a child of any age once he or she has the ability to write sentences.

We give young people a 3 x 5 inch index card, and on one side we coach them through writing a prayer they could use to open a meeting. On the reverse side, we help them develop a prayer they could use to end a meeting. We instruct students to keep the 3 x 5 card in their Bible. We also ask students to transfer their opening and closing prayers onto a sheet of paper they can place in a notebook for future reference.

Then, as we simply "live out our church lives," we ask youth to take turns opening and closing our times together with prayer. Once youth become accustomed to opening and closing with prayer, they begin to forgo the 3 x 5 card and they just pray from their heart. I particularly love it when a teen volunteers to pray at an event, and I ask if he or she wants a 3 x 5 card to write a prayer on, and they sarcastically say, "Gary, I'm in 8th grade. I know how to pray!" *Yes, you do, praise God!*

Example of an Opening Prayer: *Dear Lord, thank you for giving us the opportunity to meet this evening. We ask that you bring to light what is important for us to talk about tonight. Bless our efforts as we meet to discuss your will and your work for our church. Work through us to put this broken world back together. Give us your wisdom and your guidance. In Jesus' name, we pray. Amen.*

Example of a Closing Prayer: *Father, thank you for the opportunity to serve. Help us to take the ideas shared and decisions made and make something meaningful from them. Bless the efforts of those taking the next steps. Grant that lives may be touched, enhanced, and changed for your glory. In Christ's name, we pray. Amen.*

Feeling comfortable in opening and closing meetings with prayer is just another Faith Stone we want youth to have in their Faith Bag. Another format we use to train our youth to pray is the PRAY prayer method.

PRAY prayer method

PRAY is an acronym which stands for Praise, Repent, Ask, and Yield. The PRAY method of prayer is an excellent format for youth to acquire when learning how to pray. This format can be used in either a personal prayer time or for a simple opening or closing of a meeting.

The PRAY model starts with <u>Praise</u>. Using this format youth start a prayer time by focusing on God and His goodness, rather than jumping in and giving God a bunch of requests. This is a time to thank God. It may mean listening to praise music, singing praise songs, or playing a musical instrument. It may mean reading a psalm or two or just quietly reflecting on all the good that God has done. For me, praise means slowing down, relaxing, taking a breath, and becoming still before my God. Regardless, it is a time to focus our heart on God and His character. Focusing on His character lends itself well to a one-line prayer of praise such as, "Dear God, you are awesomely powerful, kind, and gracious."

The second part of the PRAY prayer method is <u>Repent</u>. Before we start to petition God with requests, we teach youth to reflect on their relationships and draw out any unconfessed sin in their lives.

Thirdly, we ask that young people focus on <u>Ask</u>. This is a time to pray for all of the items we want to bring before God, such as school, work, relationships, family concerns, health concerns, etc. We like the PRAY model as it helps students to work through the process of praise and repentance before asking. This requires youth to take their focus off of themselves and unto God before they begin to lay their requests before Him. In this way our relationship with God is developed beyond God being a cosmic Santa Claus who is only there to meet our own personal whims and desires.

The fourth part of the PRAY model is <u>Yield</u>. We want youth to end their prayer time by acknowledging that God has their best interest at heart and to always yield to God and His will for them. They can do this by simply saying the prayer "and above all, your will be done." Overtime, this prayer can deepen to prayers of seeking and yielding to His will, trusting in His goodness and love, as well as prayers for help and equipping to do His will.

When introducing the PRAY method, we post one-line prayers around the room. After youth have had a chance to read the posted examples, students then identify which sentences specifically are prayers of Praise, Repentance, Asking, or Yielding. Afterwards, I show students how they can take any of the sentences and put them in the order of PRAY with the end result being a beautifully written prayer which can be used privately, as well as publically. Students are then well equipped to write their own PRAY prayer.

After talking about different settings where one might have the opportunity to open a meeting in prayer, I ask students to get in pairs and write a prayer using the PRAY format. Some of the settings include a 4-H meeting, a sporting event, a youth group event, a birthday party, a service trip send-off, a children's Sunday school hour, etc. After the pairs have written their prayers, we then share them with each other.

Below are some prayers written by middle school students:

- *Hi God, It's Alli. I just wanted to say that you are so amazing. You are forgiving, loving, and wise, and I know that you are always there for me. Thank you for all of the blessings that you have given us, and thank you for your unfailing love. We confess that we sin against you and are so sorry. Please bless all of our family and friends and let us glorify you at this event today. Your will be done today and always. Amen.*

- *Hi God, it's us again. We saw your grace at our event today, and you showed us again that you are with us always. Thank you for your forgiveness and for allowing us all to gather here today to learn from you. We are sorry for not appreciating everything that you give to us and for not always following in your footsteps. Please help us to be a blessing to others as we leave today and shine our lights to the world. Yours is the power and glory forever. Amen.*

- *Dear God, you are awesomely powerful, kind, and gracious. Thank you for continuing to give your grace to each of us. We confess that we fail to fully follow your ways. Bless our time this evening as we gather to plan this event. May your will be done in the lives we touch. Amen.*

- *Dear Lord, we praise you for who you are. Thank you for your presence in our lives and bless our efforts with good weather. We admit our mistakes as we plan to work together. Give us strength to do what you are calling us to do. Amen.*

Notice that the prayers follow the PRAY model exactly. Is this the only way to pray? No, but it is a good format for youth to use as a guide.

I think we would all agree that being comfortable opening and closing a meeting in prayer is a Faith Stone that every believer should have in his or her Faith Bag. The added benefit is it draws us all closer to our heavenly Father.

Faith Stone 28

Lead a Table Grace

S everal years ago, I was invited by a congregation to attend their morning worship service, share a meal together, and make a presentation on youth ministry. I arrived on time to participate in the worship service. After the worship service, the congregation moved to the fellowship hall for the meal. I was both surprised and pleased to see that 70 to 80 people stayed for the meal and presentation.

After making my way around the fellowship hall, I was anxious for the meal to start. I knew I had an hour presentation and if we were to be done and gone by 2:00 pm then I needed to start talking at 12:45 pm. I always like to be respectful of people's time. It was now noon. That meant we only had 45 minutes for our meal.

The food was ready and everyone was standing around. At first, I did not know why we were not starting to eat. The food was going to get cold, and I could tell there were quite a few hungry people in the room. Eventually, I figured out everyone was waiting for the pastor to come and give the table blessing. It appears he traditionally gave grace before every meal at church. However, on this particular Sunday, the pastor had become engaged in an important conversation with one of his parishioners after worship.

So, we waited. I watched the clock. The time was 12:04 pm, 12:08 pm, 12:11 pm. My 12:45 pm start time was now in jeopardy. At 12:15 pm, I thought to myself, *I could say the table grace*. However, I decided to wait to see what would happen. 12:18 pm, 12:21 pm. Finally at 12:26 pm the pastor came and gave the blessing and went immediately back to his conversation. Someone had actually gone and interrupted his important conversation and dragged him over to the fellowship hall just to give grace. *This is absurd,* I thought, *between seventy and eighty people waited nearly half an hour to eat because no one would stand up and say grace.* I came home that evening and told my wife, "That's it! Going forward, we are going to train every young person in our congregation to give a table blessing."

Table grace sounds like a simple concept. Yet many in congregations find it uncomfortable to say grace, especially in front of a large group of people. One of the faith skills we want to make sure that youth have in their bags is the ability to say a simple table grace.

We know that it is often easier to introduce new ideas to "younger members." Children and young adolescents just seem to be open to trying new things! So, starting with our pre-teens, we undertook the quest for every youth in our congregation to be able to say a "table grace." Thus, we give opportunity for our fifth and sixth graders to learn how to say a table grace at weekly club. Then in seventh and eighth grade we intentionally built into the ministry the table grace skill. Today, with a little coaching, nearly every student from fifth grade on up through high school is able to pray before the meal, even in front of a large group.

How do we do it? We pass out 3 x 5 inch index cards to each child. We define grace as "a prayer of gratitude said to God before eating a meal." And we ask questions about what grace looks like for them and their families. Finally, we ask children, "What kinds of things could we talk about to God when we say grace?"

Children typically say, "We want to pray for the food. We thank God for the food. We pray for the people who made the food. We pray for our families and our health. We ask God to be with us at our meal." As children share, I often write their answers on a white board.

Then, I ask children to write one or two sentences on their 3 x 5 card using the list we just created. Once everyone has a sentence or two written down, I say, "You are prepared to say grace." I ask the children, "How many people in the world do you think are about to eat lunch right now?"

They will answer, "Like millions of people!"

I say, "That's right. Do you think God can hear over a million prayers at the same time?"

They always answer, "Yes."

Then I say, "Okay, well, all of us are going to pray our prayer of grace at the same time. It may sound a little confusing to us, but it will make sense to God." I tell the children to just focus on their own prayer card. Then I say, "So, on the count of three we are all going to read our prayer cards out loud. Ready? One, two, three…" Then we read the cards together. And I mean all together, at the same time.

Actually, it is pretty neat to hear a bunch of elementary school age children all saying grace at the same moment. Over the course of time, you can begin to ease most youth into reading his or her table grace card solo in front of the group. Before too long, most children do not even need the card.

I often ask for volunteers to say grace. If the group is young and I get four children who raise their hands, then I simply have all four youth each take their turn praying. Each grace tends to be only a few seconds long, so there is no reason to pick one youth over another. We can easily listen to four different ten-second prayers before we eat. If the group is older and no one will have his or her feelings hurt, then we just choose one person. Routinely, when we have events where we will have multiple meals, we will put out a schedule and ask youth to sign up to say grace.

Finally, here's an idea for preparing youth to say a table grace at a special occasion, such as the family Thanksgiving meal. We typically introduce this idea to middle school youth at the start of the school year. We set a goal for the youth to give the table prayer for their family once during Thanksgiving weekend. We inform parents and ask for them to help decide whether this should be done in front of a small group of immediate family members or in front of the extended family. As with many of the other skills we train youth to do, we provide youth with examples, coach them through writing a rough draft Thanksgiving Day prayer, and then have them practice. Throughout the fall, we revisit and tweak the prayer. By Thanksgiving, students are prepared to say table grace at a special family meal. The Sunday after Thanksgiving it's encouraging to hear youth report back to us their experience. Youth talk about the positive comments or hugs they received from a teary-eyed family member.

When David thought about all that God had done, he responded with a grateful heart and a word of thanks on his lips. In Psalm 9:1 (NIV), David proclaims, "I will give thanks to you, Lord, with all my heart; I will tell of all your wonderful deeds." In my mind, I imagine one of the stones in David's shepherd's bag being etched with the words "give thanks." We can encourage students to engrave the words "give thanks" on one of their Faith Stones as well.

Faith Stone 29

Recognize God's Presence in the World

A nother favorite Bible passage of mine comes from I Samuel, chapter 3. At the beginning of this chapter, Samuel and his mentor, Eli, had just retired for the evening when this encounter takes place.

The lamp of God had not yet gone out, and Samuel was lying down in the house of the Lord where the ark of God was. Then the Lord called Samuel.

Samuel answered, "Here I am." And he ran to Eli and said, "Here I am; you called me."

But Eli said, "I did not call; go back and lie down." So he went back to lie down.

Again the Lord called, "Samuel!" And Samuel got up and went to Eli and said, "Here I am; you called me."

"My son," Eli said, "I did not call; go back and lie down."

Now Samuel did not yet know the Lord well enough to recognize his voice.

A third time the Lord called, "Samuel!" And Samuel got up and went to Eli and said, "Here I am; you called me."

Then Eli realized that the Lord was calling the boy. So Eli told Samuel, "Go and lie down, and if he calls you, say,

'Speak, Lord, for your servant is listening.'" So Samuel went and lay down in his place.

The Lord came and stood there, calling as at the other times, "Samuel! Samuel!"

Then Samuel said, "Speak, for your servant is listening."

How interesting that Samuel, in spite of being raised in the Temple, did not recognize the voice of God. The story reminds me of many of the young people I encounter. They are young men and women raised in the church, yet they do not recognize God in their everyday lives. How sad and how tragic for this to be the case.

I believe there is an "art" to listening to the voice of God, to hearing, seeing, and recognizing God in our everyday lives. God is speaking; do we have ears to hear? For most of us, acquiring this skill takes intentional practice. Just as it takes practice and dedication to become proficient at a sport or playing a musical instrument, we need to intentionally practice hearing and seeing God in our lives.

It is also important to help students recognize and trust in God's voice and character. We have talked about the broken world, how God redeems the broken world, and how we are called to be His hands and feet in helping piece a broken world back together. But when a student is experiencing the brokenness that life brings, it becomes important to remind him or her of God's character and His presence in his or her life. Otherwise, students can easily get lost in the broken-ness. Being human beings, who live on this planet, we cannot escape the ramifications of brokenness. We will experience pain, loss, and sickness. We will grieve over the death of a loved one. We need a place to hang our hope and place our trust. When the world doesn't make sense and brokenness seems overwhelming, where do we go? Thank the Lord! We can count on God and His never changing character. Hebrews 13:8 reminds us that "Jesus Christ is the same yesterday, today, and forever." James 1:17 echoes that thought by proclaiming "every good and perfect gift is from above, coming down from the Father of the heavenly lights, who does not change like shifting shadows." It is on this character that David placed his hope when he exclaimed, "The battle is the Lord's!" (I Samuel 17:47) Recognizing God and placing our trust in His character is a faith skill every student needs in his or her bag.

A few years back, my wife and I were with another couple at a shopping mall. As we were strolling by the shops, a kiosk in the middle of the walkway caught our attention. This kiosk was selling something I had never seen before. Hanging on the booth's walls were assorted framed pictures. I did not know it at the time, but I was looking at a new product called a stereogram. Merriam-Webster dictionary defines a stereogram as "a diagram or picture representing objects with an impression of solidity or relief." Evidently, there was a 3-D image hidden in each of the pictures. From my point of view, it was a set up for a practical joke.

What I observed were about twenty people gathered around the kiosk intently looking at the designs in the framed pictures. Interested participants were putting their noses close to the picture frame and slowly backing the frame away, fixating their eyes deep into the design. Every once in a while, someone would exclaim, "Oh, I see it!" Quite baffled, I thought, *Hmm, see what?*

It didn't take long for my wife and our friends to become intrigued and fully engaged in the search for the unknown images. They had picture frames in hand and were looking intently into the pictures. I, on the other hand, remained skeptical and wary. I deduced not only was this a hoax, but we were victims of an elaborate "candid camera" television scheme. I actually kept my distance from the cart so as not to be "seen on camera."

After a few minutes, my wife gave a shout, "Oh, I see it! It's the Starship Enterprise!" Knowing my wife would not make up something like that, I ventured closer to the vendor. Tentatively, I made my way toward a framed image. I peered into the picture looking for a hidden message in what was otherwise a non-descript bunch of colored squiggly lines.

Minutes passed. Soon our friends were also making the cry, "I see it!" Replanting my feet and gripping the frame, I tried harder. Certainly, if there was something there to see, I would eventually see it. But, my companions tired of the activity, and we moved on.

I never did see any images that day, but over the next few weeks, stereogram pictures started showing up everywhere, even in the comics section of the Sunday paper. So, in the privacy of my home, I spent considerable time attempting to see through the design for the deeper level. Yep, it took a while, but I eventually did see the image. Over the next few weeks, I took every opportunity that came my way and I focused on the pictures until I saw the image. Today, I can pick up a stereogram and see the 3-D hidden image within seconds.

Several years ago, at our elementary school age camp, we used a curriculum that introduced the concept of God sightings. Throughout the weekend, children were asked, "Where did you see God today?"

It was not a new idea to us. Years before this camp experience, we actually had been asking this question with our high school youth. We would open high school Bible study with students sharing their weekly highs, lows, and God sightings. It was also a common practice during the high school Sunday school class. Students were easily able to identify highs and lows, but it took time for them to identity God sightings. We repeatedly did lessons on the topic, defining what a God sighting was and what it might look like.

So, when my wife and I came back from that weekend camp experience, we were excited that the concept of God sightings had been introduced to the younger children. We were curious to see how this newly founded knowledge would play out back in the congregation. We went into a full court blitz of adding the "God sighting" term all throughout the ministry.

The next summer, God sightings were again a part of the weekend programming at camp. Our older teens stood in front of the camp and shared personal stories of times they had seen God in their lives. These stories revealed God's goodness and faithfulness. It was at the closing finale at camp when children came forward to sing songs and share their highlights of the weekend that we heard children for the first time use the wording, *"My God sighting* this weekend was..." After we came home from camp and reflected on the weekend, we realized all those years of talking about God sightings with high school students and all the teaching and repetition with the younger children finally came to fruition over the weekend. It was worth it.

Since then, we have heard the term "God sighting" shared from adults in our church and even from the pulpit. Today, you can ask most of the active students in the congregation where they saw God this week; to our delight, we often get deep, meaningful, and profound answers.

On September 11, 2001, I lost a cousin in tower #2. I waited, along with family members, for news about Derek. I went to the website of the company he worked for to see if his name was still listed among the missing. I thought of his wife, Kim, and their young son. Derek and Kim were also expecting their second child.

What does one do in the midst and aftermath of such tragedy? People of faith see God. As others were asking and struggling in the days, months, and years to follow, with the question, "Where was God on September 11, 2001?" Derek's wife, Kim, was seeing God. Over the course of the next few years, both on television and in magazine interviews, Kim talked about seeing God's faithfulness throughout the experience. Kim saw God in the life of her husband, through the legacy of her children, and through her new found desire to go back to school to become a spiritual director so she could help others through tragedy. Throughout the years, Kim talked about the redeeming blessings that come from knowing God. Her ability to see God in the darkest of times has given her, and many others, the courage and strength to face each new day.

God is active and at work in our lives, yet I wonder how many of us miss the blessings of seeing God and His character unveiled around us each day. Training students to recognize God in their lives is a worthwhile goal and, surely, a Faith Stone we want them to have in their Faith Bag. Please train your children and youth to recognize God in their everyday lives. He is there. One just has to have "eyes to see."

Faith Stone 30

Verbalize the Faith

Verbalizing our faith helps to solidify what we believe. Who gets the most out of teaching Sunday school? The Sunday school teacher! The presenter probably gets the most out of the VBS lesson. And dare I say, yep, the pastor probably gets the most out of the sermon. I can say that because I believe I get the most out of the presentations I make. The presenter spends so much time preparing, it just makes sense that he/she will get the most out of his/her presentation. Learning to verbalize your faith is the first step towards being able to share your faith with others, teach others, and enhance your understanding of what you believe. Therefore, we believe it is important to intentionally train youth how to verbalize their faith.

One of the ways we help our students verbalize their faith is to have each young person during their middle school years develop a faith tri-fold. *What's a faith tri-fold?* Think of a science fair display constructed of corrugated cardboard, about a yard high with three panels on it. Actually, I like to refer to this tri-fold display as a faith-fold, as on its three sections students express important elements of their faith. The faith-fold becomes a tool students can refer to when they first formally practice talking about their faith with others.

In the spring of their eighth grade year, students begin the process of creating their personalized faith-fold. It can take more than six months for students to complete the process of creating, developing, and then actually talking about the faith topics posted on their faith-fold. The goal is for each student to be equipped and ready to verbalize his or her faith at their Faith Celebration, which takes place in the fall of a student's freshmen year in high school. We call it Faith Celebration, as we are celebrating each student's faith journey and giving them opportunity to share their faith with others.

During the faith-fold process, youth pick a theme for their faith-fold, identify topics that have helped to form their faith foundation, develop and write stories on each of the topics, create their presentation on their faith-fold, and then spend time learning how to talk about those faith topics. It sounds like a lot, but once the project gets underway, teens typically really get into the project.

The topics students choose for their faith-fold usually center around their Baptism, statement of faith, favorite service project, favorite Bible story, verse or character, a God sighting, and/or their faith web. Each section is personalized through their own faith experiences.

> To connect with Gary about the Faith-Fold
> Process visit www.faithwebbing.com

We introduce the concept late winter of a student's 8th grade school year. Young people then spend the next three or four months thinking through their faith-folds. Over the summer they narrow down and choose a theme and design a plan for what they want their faith-fold to look like. They continue to develop the sections of the faith-fold throughout the summer months. Then, in early fall, they put the finishing touches on their project. Next, they begin to practice their presentations. For several weeks in Sunday school, we bring in a different set of folks to hear youth practice their presentations. We especially make sure that the younger grades get a chance to hear the presentations.

Then, in late October comes the night of the Faith Celebration. Tables are set up in our Family Life Center. Faith-folds are sprinkled throughout the room. Colorful balloons, upbeat background music, and festive snacks set the tone for the evening. Students stand next to their faith-folds. The room is alive with conversation. As you walk around, you can listen to students as they share God sightings, their favorite service project, important people in their faith web, their favorite Bible verse or story, and why their faith is important to them. It's one of my favorite nights of the year; a night when students talk about faith, and not just faith, but their personal faith in our living Triune God.

With this system, youth practice their presentations a dozen or more times before the night of the Faith Celebration and at the Celebration they make their presentations at least another dozen times. By the end of the evening, youth have shared their faith in a church setting over two dozen times. This is a great training method. Students have developed a faith, written out a statement of faith, identified key elements that have enhanced their faith, and then they have practiced sharing their faith. As a result, they are prepared for opportunities to share their faith outside of the church walls.

Being able to verbalize faith is a wonderful skill for a young person to have in their bag. It is a skill that helps students to answer the questions they get from friends. Questions like...

Why do you go to church? They can answer, "Let me tell you about Phil…"

Why do you go to Bible Study? They can answer, "Let me tell you about my favorite Bible story…"

Why are you going on a church trip? They can answer, "Let me tell you about the homeless shelter I went to…"

Why do you believe in God? They can answer by sharing their faith web, their "I believe" statement, or a God sighting.

Todd was a young man who grew up in our congregation. As a sophomore in high school, Todd invited a friend of his named Will to attend church events. Will soon was attending everything he could and after a couple of years he followed through on his new found faith by becoming baptized. Over the years, I got to know Will pretty well.

When Will was in his early twenties, I had a conversation with him about his faith walk. Will described how he started attending church because of Todd. He mentioned how impressed he was in high school with Todd's faith. Will went on to say that Todd's confidence in his faith, his ability to express his faith, and Todd's thoughts on why church was important to him gave Will the desire to come to church. I can't help but think that Todd's faith-fold experience helped him to be able to verbalize his faith, which in turn led to Todd eventually inviting his friend Will to church.

How cool is that? *Is learning how to verbalize your faith a faith stone worth having in your bag?* Ask Will, who now has a new found relationship with Jesus.

A Cultural Cycle of Training

―――――ᒐᗺ―――――

Before I was born the Lord called me; from my mother's womb he has spoken my name. He made my mouth like a sharpened sword, in the shadow of his hand he hid me; he made me into a polished arrow and concealed me in his quiver.
He said to me, "You are my servant, Israel, in whom I will display my splendor." (Isaiah 49:1-3, NIV)

Our charge is to help our children and youth become polished arrows; polished arrows hidden in a quiver to be sent out to the right place, at the right time, by the Lord God Almighty for His glory. Whoa, that's pretty deep. But isn't that what we as a church are all about; helping youth to develop their personal relationship with Jesus as we equip them for a lifetime of service to Christ? As we take seriously the concept

> **Our charge is to help our children and youth become polished arrows.**

of outcome-based youth ministry, our definition of youth ministry changes. The new definition of youth ministry becomes "Youth Ministry is Youth <u>Doing</u> Ministry."

In doing so, we get the privilege of training youth in acquiring ministry skills chosen by them. We then get to watch as youth put their newly acquired skills into action. Over time, youth become competent in their chosen areas even to the point that they begin to train others to follow in their footsteps. An effectual cultural cycle of choosing, learning, implementing, and then training others in Faith Skills is established. Youth respond positively to the process and look forward to the day when they get to train and lead others. It is a win-win scenario for all involved.

As children grow and develop, they strive for independence and identity. This can manifest itself through identifying individual gifts, talents, and interests. Congregations can then offer opportunities for youth to express themselves and their faith through these new found attributes. The goal is to give youth a path to explore their interests in a loving, caring, faith-based environment.

When Mindy was in fifth grade, she wandered into my office and said, "Gary, I want to lead a service project." That may sound odd, but in the culture we have created in our congregation, it was a normal and natural request. We had spent years not just involving youth in churchwide service projects, but encouraging them to share project ideas with us that they themselves wanted to lead. If the idea was feasible, we would figure out a way to "coach" him or her through the project. That's what I was hoping to do with Mindy's request. So, searching my mind for a project idea, I remembered a flier that had come across my desk earlier in the week. It was for something called "Souper Bowl Sunday." The project was new to me. When I revisited the flier, I saw the Souper Bowl project was a nationwide, student-led effort to raise funds for a local food pantry or soup kitchen during the weekend of the NFL Super Bowl. "Hmm," I thought, "putting money in a soup kettle to feed the hungry in our community. This might work."

I introduced the idea to Mindy, and she took to it right away. We met throughout the fall months and I began to "coach" Mindy through the process of starting a new ministry in the congregation. We presented the idea to the social ministry committee, gaining their approval. I helped Mindy understand how to publicize and communicate the project through the weekly bulletin and monthly newsletter. We talked about how to give an announcement during worship and how to recruit others to be involved. We went through every detail, even discussing where to find the soup kettles on collection day.

When Super Bowl Sunday arrived, Mindy had her team in place. Youth stood at the doors of the church and collected money after each worship service. Coins could be heard clinking throughout the church as they made their way to the bottom of each kettle. That afternoon, Mindy and I met and discussed how to count the money, how to get the money to the folks that recorded and deposited funds, and then how to request a check to be sent to the local food pantry. Once the check was sent, we developed a brief report to document the service project and then filed the report away for the next year.

Whew, a lot went into taking a simple offering for a food pantry, but Mindy took on every aspect of the project with enthusiasm. By the time the project ended, Mindy had collected over $500. What a great learning experience, and Mindy loved it. There was no way she was not going to lead the Souper Bowl project again next year. She was hooked.

The second year, Mindy and I initiated "the next step." Instead of just sending a check to the food pantry, Mindy called the pantry and asked for a list of food items that were in short supply. With shopping list in hand, Mindy recruited several others to go shopping with her. Imagine eight middle school students, at the grocery store, paired up in four teams, and each pair with a clipboard, shopping list, pencil, calculator, and $125 in hand. They were ready to shop for the food pantry. The youth loved the experience. Before heading back to church, we unloaded the food at the food pantry and took a ten minute tour. The youth left the pantry knowing they are an important piece of a bigger picture in fighting hunger. It was a good experience for all.

The first year Mindy and I did the project together; it was about 85% me and 15% Mindy. The second year, using her notes from the previous year, the experience was closer to 50% me and 50% Mindy. By her seventh grade year, Mindy was handling most of the project by herself. And, by her freshman year in high school, the project was all Mindy. By this point, all I needed to do was ask her if she wanted to do the project again, hand her the Souper Bowl file, and provide her some accountability and support. I just had to ask an occasional question. Mindy ran the project for eight years. In that time period, I'm happy to note that Mindy collected over $6,000 for the local food pantry.

Knowing Mindy was likely to go to an out-of-state college after graduating from high school, I suggested in her junior year that she choose a protégée, someone she could train to take over the ministry. After shadowing Mindy for two years, Wendy was prepared to take on the project. Now, years later, our congregation still does Souper Bowl Sunday, and it is still run by a young person. What a great ministry. And to think, it all started with one young fifth grade girl and her desire to serve others, a desire that eventually involved an entire congregation and turned into an ongoing ministry.

Yep, it takes a good deal of time to coach a young person through a project, but that's what faith coaching is all about, and it can pay off big time in the long run. As seen in Mindy, a single life can make a difference in the lives of many.

Developing specific ministry skills in youth is another forum where many of the precepts in this book come together. Understanding the message of the Gospel, the Acts 1:8 service philosophy, and having developed the other spiritual disciplines in a young person's life helps him or her to understand the need for service and sacrifice. Having a grasp on personality temperaments, love languages, and spending time with people the way Jesus did helps young people to work well with others. Being able to properly introduce yourself, having personal written standards to live by, and having a Biblical self-esteem gives young people the confidence to step out in faith. Then having a well-developed Faith Web gives youth the network they need to take on bigger projects and flourish where they are planted. It takes many skill sets to pull off big projects. It is our job to equip young people with the necessary skill sets they will need to live out their faith.

Having an abundance of skills in a young person's bag makes deeper ministry possible. The more Faith Stones that have been developed and placed in a young person's Faith Bag, the more prepared he or she will be to do ministry.

We consider ourselves at St. John's to be a training ground for Christian youth. We want to create an atmosphere and culture where young people learn the necessary faith disciplines so that they can walk with God all the days of their lives. We also want them to discover their individual gifts, talents, and interests, and then we wish to provide opportunities for them to put their faith into action in these areas. We strive to create an environment where we, as leaders, can coach young people through their chosen activities while being surrounded by love and affirmation. Simply put, we want to become a training ground where youth ministry becomes youth doing ministry.

Youth grow in faith as they get a chance to shine for Jesus! Here are a few more stories of youth shining for Jesus.

Coaching Youth through an Interest: John

From experience, we have learned that giving youth the opportunity and responsibility to use a gift or skill in ministry does wonders for their faith development, their self-esteem, and their continued attendance. One way to make this a reality is to coach youth according to their interests, such as leading a service project, a worship song, a craft, a skit, a game, or a Bible lesson. Once given the opportunity to learn a new skill, a student can watch it modeled by a seasoned mentor, and then be coached by that seasoned mentor when it is their turn to put their newly found skill into practice.

I once led a workshop on involving children and youth in ministry. A group of twenty-five people from a half dozen congregations came to brainstorm ways to involve youth in church. We decided to start with worship. We asked the question, "In what ways can we involve our children and youth in weekly worship?" Seventy-five minutes later, I told the group we had to move on to another topic. There were so many ideas flowing through the room, it was hard to keep up with it all. Our young people are gifted and talented and there are many ways to take their individual gifts, talents, and interests and involve them in meaningful ministry.

Here is an example:

John is standing with guitar in hand during the music time at our weekly elementary club. John is in third grade. He's up front with the other guitar players as parents, grandparents, and siblings arrive knowing "something's up." John is making his BIG debut even though he has only been playing guitar for one month and only knows the chord of "C." He is intently staring at his music, watching for his BIG moment to play the "C" chord. Throughout the entire song he plays only one chord multiple times. Family and friends erupt in applause. John feels competent, affirmed, and successful. Within a month, he'll be playing two chords, then three, and eventually many more chords. By the time he is in high school, John will be teaching a younger youth how to play guitar.

About a month earlier, John had expressed an interest in learning how to play guitar. We offered him free guitar lessons on the condition that he would play in front of the group as soon as he mastered one or two chords. It is not uncommon for us to have a bunch of guitar players at various levels of expertise playing in front of a group. We have also used this concept with various other instruments. Some years we have quite a hodgepodge of musicians up front. These are all youth being given opportunity to display their interests in a ministry setting. They love it, parents love it, and faith develops.

Do we need guitar players? Yes, we do. But so much more goes into the guitar learning experience. One of the main goals was actually realized in the faith webbing that took place between John and Alan. Alan was the high school guy who met with John for 30 minutes each week to teach him a chord or two. Regardless of where the guitar lessons led, John will always have a relationship with Alan, because Alan has become a significant person in John's faith web. In addition, Alan got to know John's parents. As a result of Alan's kindness, John's parents financially helped Alan attend a summer church camp. Alan's parents thanked John's parents for helping their son go to church camp. As a result, two families have formed a deeper friendship.

During this experience, John also connected with several other high school age guitar players who all treated him with kindness and affirmation. Younger youth saw John playing guitar in front of the group and some asked if they could also play their instrument during the opening of club. Good things happened all around.

Coaching Youth through an Interest: Andrew

A middle school student named Andrew came up to me one day and asked if the youth group could go bowling. You see, Andrew was an avid bowler. I replied, "Yes, but you're in charge."

His face lit up. "What does that mean?" he asked. I told him it meant that he would be the leader, but I would coach him through putting the event together.

We started by selecting a bowling alley and a date for the event. Andrew knew the local lanes well and immediately suggested we use the small eight-lane location within walking distance of the church. As we talked, he also decided to hold the event during a regular youth group meeting time. He figured it would help attendance if the event was held when we typically met. Next, I told him we would need to think about getting another couple of people to help plan the event, and think through advertising, possible transportation, permission slips, adult help, food, and maybe music. Andrew was off and running with his idea.

Over the next couple of weeks Andrew and I connected on the progress of the planning. He involved a friend in the planning, had good ideas, and I helped him to stay focused and make good decisions by asking questions.

Here is what Andrew put together:

The middle school youth group met at the church that Wednesday evening and with permission slips in hand, they began to be shuttled the half mile to the Bowling Alley. Andrew was there to greet everyone, and he assigned them to bowling lanes. He took into consideration which students were friends and he made sure best friends were kept together. Next, with my help, he assigned a high school student to each lane. His or her main responsibility was to add fun and enthusiasm to the lane, thus ensuring everyone had a positive experience. Lastly, we assigned an adult to each lane to just watch the lane and whoop, holler and cheer every ball that was bowled. The cheering adults also kept the pizzas and pop coming.

Oh yeah, before starting, we called the group together and told them it was to be a team competition and we were all on the same team. He asked each lane to add up their bowling averages and the goal for each lane was to beat their averages. In this way we were all working together and not rooting against each other.

It was a quick 90 minute activity. About twenty youth, five high school students and five adults were present. The evening went really well and I made sure everyone knew that Andrew put the event together. He became the hero. He beamed.

Andrew's goal was to go bowling. My goal was to match Andrew's passion of bowling with a project, hoping to equip him along the way. I wanted to teach him how to plan an event, think through details, and develop good decision-making skills. Throughout this process we wanted to stay true to the culture we had created of being a loving, caring intergenerational community based on affirmation and support. And, in the end, my goal was to make the young person the "hero."

This scenario can be played out with other interests as well. Learning how to lead songs, perform skits, lead games, make snacks, and create crafts are all important elements to our church ministries. Helping youth become competent in these areas builds skills that can be used not only in congregational programming today but throughout their lives. In the implementation and practice of skills, opportunities present themselves to deepen youth's relationship with their Creator and others. An added benefit is their self-esteem heightens through these new skills.

Through it all, the underlying emphasis is furthering relationships. With a focus on developing long-term nurturing relationships with young people, the door opens to all kinds of faith skills training. The overall ministry then becomes a relational training ground where young people explore newly discovered gifts and talents. In our congregation, we are always training a new crop of youth who are developing ministry skills. Ministry skills we hope they will continue to utilize at their church of attendance when they become adults.

We have a defined vision, we are prepared, and we are intentional in all that we do. In our culture of outcome-based youth ministry, we are creating a culture of youth *doing* ministry.

It may be helpful to point out that our weekly programs are neither well-rehearsed nor flashy. That is by design. Our events highlight lots of young people dabbling in interests and displaying new talents. When visitors attend, they are impressed with the ratio of leaders to youth (often times the ratio is actually one-to-one) and with the amount of love and attention given to each child. However, visitors also leave with the thought, "we could do that," which would be a correct assumption on their part. One of our goals is to create a systematic ministry that can be replicated in most other congregations. Our intention is not to impress, but to quietly, unassumingly, and humbly equip and train the next generation of believers so that they may have a plethora of Faith Stones in their Faith Bags.

The Visionary Notebook

I noticed throughout our beginning years in youth ministry that much of what we hoped to pass on to youth through church experiences was good for the day, the week, the month, or the school year, but didn't seem to take hold as much as we hoped. Yes, some students were able to retain and apply these skills for life. For others, though, much got lost in the day-to-day struggles and busyness of life. How could we get more of these Faith Stone concepts to stick, grow, and develop for the long haul?

I began to realize that youth needed a framework for the discipleship skills they were learning. They needed a place to record experiences, organize written thoughts and to store lessons learned for future reference on matters of faith. They needed a place to compile written hopes, goals, and dreams for the future. The Visionary Notebook is a tool we have developed to meet that need.

The Visionary Notebook is a three ring binder that corresponds with the Faith Stones we teach. It is a place for young people to store virtually every handout we give them from middle school through high school. It has tabs to help them keep, organize, and be able to refer back to every SOAP sheet, those extensive thankful lists, their written standards to live by, purpose prayers, devotional worksheets, representations of their Faith Webs, etc.

The Visionary Notebook has become much more than just a notebook to store papers. We have found that the Visionary Notebook becomes uniquely personal for each individual as he or she chooses to use it as...

- a diary where youth can place their most intimate thoughts, ideas, and feelings
- a scrapbook where youth can store awards, ribbons, certificates of achievement, grade cards, etc.
- a place to keep lists, written standards to live by, financial goals, documentation of service experiences and ministry plans or
- a prayer manual where youth may pray through goals, hopes, and dreams for life, as well as include photos of people who are important to them

The Visionary Notebook is both a resource and a tool to be used throughout the development of a young person's life, ultimately helping them grow a faith-based hope and a vision for the future.

More than anything, I consider the Visionary Notebook project to be a journey. It is a creative process which evolves over time as a young person prayerfully considers and discerns God's call in his or her life.

We give a Visionary Notebook to each young person as he or she begins middle school, and in our ministry we add to the notebook regularly. Each and every month, we have multiple items that we add to or update in the notebooks. We revisit the notebook often.

It is my sincere prayer each student I work with develops a Visionary Notebook which becomes a living, breathing, working tool integrating life and faith for ongoing lifelong discipleship.

Are your wheels turning yet? Consider this...

Imagine your students having their very own Visionary Notebooks containing everything you have taught them over the last few years. Imagine youth showing up to class or events with a notebook in hand that is bulging at the seams. Imagine teens asking to get together with you to further develop specific sections of their notebooks. Imagine that by the time students graduate from high school, they have outgrown the one inch binder you gave them and their Visionary Notebook library is now made up of three or four notebooks. Imagine adults in their 20s and 30s connecting with you and telling you how they are currently utilizing their notebook in their faith journey.

Yep, I experience the above on a regular basis.

> **If you are interested in the Visionary Notebook concept, contact Gary through www.faithwebbing.com**

Conclusion

———◦◜◝◦———

I n Luke, Jesus sends his disciples out in pairs to the surrounding towns and villages. "Take nothing for your journey," he instructed them. "Don't take a walking stick, a traveler's bag, food, money, or even a change of clothes." Was Jesus really sending his beloved disciples out into the world without anything? No. He had been preparing them for quite some time for what they would encounter when they went out into the world to share his Father's message of repentance. He had filled their Faith Bags with the necessary Faith Stones. They needed nothing else.

David, when he faced Goliath, had all that he needed in his bag to win the victory over the Philistines. He not only had a bag full of throwing stones and a sling, he had a heart for God and a faith bigger than Goliath. He needed nothing else.

Examples of ordinary people doing extraordinary things abound in the Bible. Whatever the task presented to them, they had in their Faith Bags what they needed to accomplish the task and glorify the Father.

God is constantly placing and positioning us for His glory. When a mission needs to be accomplished, our Lord looks across the land to find a believer with both the faith and the skill to accomplish the task at hand. Sometimes, it is to visit an elderly person in an assisted care facility and share a kind word and prayer. Sometimes, it is to preach the

Gospel boldly to ears primed to hear. Sometimes, it is to be the leader and demonstrate how faith shapes our lives and sometimes, yes sometimes, it is to take on a giant.

Youth, equipped with bags full of faith stones and the understanding that the battle belongs to God, can face whatever comes their way. Like the disciples being sent out, we are sending our young people into the world with what they need to share their faith and face the giants. They have God in their hearts and skills in their bag. They need nothing else.

God's blessings to you and your young people as you strive to become God's workmanship, created in Christ Jesus to do good works, which God prepared in advance for you to do. With our bags in hand, may we be a blessing to others.

Contact Page

About the Author

Gary Pecuch can be reached at www.faithwebbing.com, and he invites you to connect with him as you ponder the ideas presented in this book, or if you feel you would like some assistance implementing these ideas.

Gary is a writer, speaker, trainer, faith coach, workshop leader, retreat leader, and story teller. His mission is to train and equip God's people with the necessary Faith Skills to live out their personal calling in life.

Gary offers a variety of programming for both adults and youth and is willing to travel for presentations and speaking engagements. Below is a list of topics on which Gary speaks most.

- Creating a healthy youth ministry culture in your congregation.

- Faith Webbing: wrapping your children and youth in a web of faith.

- Outcome-Based Youth Ministry: building faith skills into young people. Gary has developed and

is prepared to build into God's people various Faith
Skill sets.

- Congregational Next Steps: helping congregations to
  evaluate their current status for children and youth
  ministry and then develop next step plans for moving
  forward.

- Bible Stories: Gary has 50 Bible stories ready to go
  for talks and lessons.

- Trot through the Bible Course: a Bible course
  designed to trot 5th through 8th graders through the
  Old or New Testament in a weekend or week-long
  experience.

- Personality Temperaments: Gary acquired his
  Personality Temperament Certification from Keirsey.
  com. Understanding the basics of personality temperaments will help youth to understand their place
  in this world.

Gary has been in congregational ministry since 1982.
He holds a Bachelor of Science Degree in Administration of
Justice (Juvenile Justice) and he earned a Master's of Arts
Degree in Nonprofit Administration and Management.

Gary has written a book entitled *Faith Webbing* (Xulon
Press) and has led workshops for Group Publishing, Inc. He
has been a speaker in both college and seminary settings and
has been a speaker/presenter in hundreds of congregations.

Gary was also the Director of the Animal and Nature
Assisted Therapy Department (Equestrian Center) at the
Buckeye Ranch, Grove City, Ohio. He and his wife Laurie
were a Licensed Therapeutic Treatment Care Foster Home
for ten years.

For fun, Gary spent 20 years teaching teenagers how to drive.

Gary is passionate about passing on the Christian Faith through education and training and after 30+ years of ministry, he continues to add Faith Stones to his Faith Bag.

APPENDIX

Everyday Prayer Sheet

SOAP Sheet

The Christian View of Finances Sheet

The Financial Goals & Action Sheet

My Lenten Sacrifice Sheet

Thankful List Sheet

Thankful List Reflective Questions

Introductory Story Talk Sheet

Devotions Worksheet

EVERYDAY PRAYER SHEET

- Good morning God. I am your child. Show me your way today.
- Speak to me in a way I can understand.
- I pray for your wisdom, your guidance, and your perceptiveness in making decisions today.
- I pray I will be a blessing to others…
- I pray for my potential spouse…
- I pray for my family…

Now add your own thoughts to the list…

- _____
- _____
- _____
- _____
- _____
- _____
- _____
- _____
- _____
- _____

And above all, I pray for your will to be done in my life. Amen.

SOAP SHEET

DATE: ____________

Dear God, open our hearts and minds to your word. May it help us to grow in wisdom, and in stature, and in favor with You and others. We want to be Luke 2:52 men and women of God. Amen!

Scripture:

Observations:

Application(s):

Prayers:

Praise – God, thank you for____________________________

Repent – God, I'm so sorry for_________________________.

Ask – God, please _________________________.

Yield – Lord, not my will, but Your will be done.

Amen.

The Christian View of Finances Sheet

#1: God (owns) it all: "The earth is the (Lord's), and all it contains, the (world) and those who dwell in it." (Psalm 24:1, NASB)

#2: We are to (manage) what God has given us: "Let a man regard us in this manner, as (servants) of Christ, and (stewards) of the mysteries of God." (I Corinthians 4:1, NASB)

#3: Jesus spoke more about (money) than anything else. That means money must be extremely (important) in our (relationship) with God.

#4: It is the (love) of money and not money itself that is the (root) of all evil: Loving money leads to dishonesty, greed, deception, and hoarding. (I Timothy 6:10)

#5: In the (Old) Testament it is written we should give (10%) of the money that passes through our hands back to God. (Malachi 3:10) That's a good place to start.

#6: In the (New) Testament the message is we are to acknowledge not only does God own it all, we are to (center) everything we have been given around the cause of Christ (our time , our money, our possessions.) Remember, God owns it all. We are to be good stewards of what God has given us and we are to disperse it according to His will. (Matthew 6:19-34, Matthew 19:16-30)

#7: Our ultimate (purpose) in life is to have a right relationship with our Creator (glorify God) and to (positively) influence those we come in contact with for Christ.

Thus, our financial goals should reflect a Christian World view. With every dollar that passes through our hands, we should ask the question, "How can I use this dollar to better my relationship with God and/or help to better someone else's relationship with God?"

Therefore, giving funds to Christian causes should be a main priority in our financial planning.

You will have lots of money pass through your hands during your lifetime, most likely millions of dollars. Disperse them wisely.

#8: It is better to (give) than to (receive). The world tells us we benefit when we receive something. However, Jesus turns that thinking upside down and says those who give benefit more than those who receive. The benefit is not the reason we give; however, we serve a God who honors our giving.

The Financial Goals & Action Sheet

Start at an early age. "Train up a child in the way he should go, even when he is old he will not depart from it." (Proverbs 22:6, NASB)

Here's a good budget guideline to use through high school. Feel free to design your own. When a dollar comes your way, divide it into five different portions:

10% in the offering plate (Do this weekly.)
5% to a Christian cause (Choose causes in advance that are important to you.)
10% set aside towards retirement (You will be "big time glad" that you did.)
60% in savings for large future expenses (short or long term goals)
15% discretionary spending

List possible sources and (amounts) of income for this year:

_____
_____
_____
_____

Using the budget guideline above for this year, how much can you put towards:

Your church: _____
Other Christian causes: _____
Your retirement account: _____
Your savings account: _____
Your personal spending: _____

Ask God for wisdom and guidance in making financial decisions and consider adding your financial goals to your everyday prayer sheet.

As a start, this year I plan to give away

$ _____ to _____
$ _____ to _____
$ _____ to _____
$ _____ to _____
$ _____ to _____

MY LENTEN SACRIFICE

LENT
- 40 days between Ash Wednesday and Easter
- Time to think about our sinful self and to repent from our sins
- Time to walk with Jesus, leading up to the cross and the resurrection
- Time we remember what Jesus has done for us and how much He loves us
- Time for sacrifice!

1. Give it up! ————→ **SACRIFICE**

- Chocolate or sweets
- Chips or unhealthy food
- Pizza
- Pop
- Social Media
- Cell Phone Time
- iPod

What is important to me or something I want to change? It should be important to you. Challenging but not overwhelming. Write it on the line below:

_____

2. Trade it! ————————→ **FAITH OR SERVICE**

What preoccupies my time? What do I spend a lot of time doing that might keep me from growing in my faith or helping others?

- Give up 20 minutes of social media every day and (trade it) by reading my Bible.
- Give up 10 minutes of video games and (trade it) by praying before going to bed.
- Give up 10 minutes of music and (trade it) by loading the dishwasher.
- Give up cell phone use for 20 minutes a day and (trade it) by adding to your thankful list.

Spend less time doing your favorite activity: _____

So I can do more:

- Bible reading
- Praying (thankful list, photos in visionary notebook)
- Devotions (SOAP)
- Memorizing the books of the Bible
- Memorizing scripture
- Singing of worship songs
- Spending time with a sibling or other family member
- Folding clothes/sweep the floor, etc.
- Loading the dishwasher/empty the dishwasher
- Posting notes around the house (encouragement or thanks)
- Spending less on specialty drinks & give to a worthy cause (malaria nets)

Spend more time doing: _____, _____,
_____, _____,

3. Add something! (daily or weekly) ⟶ **WITNESS, SHOW GOD'S LOVE**

Add (for example):

- Bake cookies and give them away.
- Organize a closet and put items in the Salvation Army bin.
- Play your instrument at a nursing home.
- Take a walk and pray for your neighbors.
- Make an Easter Banner for church.
- Learn to crochet or knit for the prayer shawl ministry.
- Write an affirmation note to someone telling them how you see God in them and thanking them for being in your faith web.
- Write down a bible verse and post it in your locker for you and your friends to see.
- Watch the news and pray for the people involved.
- Start recycling.
- Journal and listen to God.
- Play a game with your family.
- Say only positive affirming things all day long.
- Add to your thankful list every day.
- Pray for your parents.

- Pray for your future potential spouse.
- Smile and say hi to the student at school who needs encouragement.
- Deliver beds with the bed brigade.

How can I live out my faith so others know His love? Write it on the line below:

_____

Things that will help you:

- Write it down.
- Tell someone.
- Do the Lenten vow with others.
- Be at worship.
- Pray about it. Ask the Holy Spirit to help you.
- Ask someone to pray for you.
- If you forget or mess up, talk to Jesus. And start again!
- Remember Jesus' sacrifice.
- Look forward to Easter.

<u>Right now I'm leaning more towards (circle one):</u>

Giving something up   Trading it

Adding something   A combination of the three

THANKFUL LIST

Thank the Lord because He is good.
His love continues forever. (Psalm 107:1)
So let us be thankful because we have a kingdom that
cannot be shaken. (Hebrews 12:28)
I thank my God every time I remember you. (Phil 1:3)

Make a list of things and people for which you are thankful.

Thankful Session Reflective Questions

Colors make the world fun and unique.

What's your favorite color?

Where do you see your favorite color?

Add to your thankful list your favorite color and anything that you can think of that is your favorite color.

Thankful Session Reflective Questions

Think about people who are important to you and your faith.

People, of all ages, whose faith you admire...

Add their names to your thankful list.

Thankful Session Reflective Questions

Families come in all different sizes and each is unique.

Family is where we learn to love, forgive, and live.

God likes families.

Add some family names to your thankful list.

(i.e. grandparents, aunts, uncles, parents, siblings, cousins, god-parents, and people who are like family to you)

<u>Thankful Session Reflective Questions</u>

Think of all the "stuff" you have that makes you happy.

We have "stuff" for comfort, necessity, fun, and even for helping others.

"Stuff" is a gift.

What items in your house are you thankful for?

Add them to you thankful list.

Thankful Session Reflective Questions

God has given you a brain and special gifts.

What do you like to do?

What would you like to learn more about?

What activities or hobbies are you involved in?

Add those things to your thankful list.

Thankful Session Reflective Questions

What sounds make you smile?

- Someone's voice?
- Laughter?
- Rain on a rooftop?
- The sound of leaves on a windy day?
- The sound of waves upon the shore?
- Encouraging words?

Think of sounds and write down ones you're thankful for...

Thankful Session Reflective Questions

What tastes good to you?

What's your favorite meal?

What special foods do you eat at holidays?

Write down foods you're thankful for...

__Thankful Session Reflective Questions__

What animals do you think are really awesome?

- In nature?
- At the zoo?
- Maybe a pet?

Add them to your thankful list.

Thankful Session Reflective Questions

What's a special memory you have with family? Or with friends?

Or perhaps a special memory of a place you've visited?

Write a word (or a short sentence) that reminds you of that time and place on your thankful list.

Thankful Session Reflective Questions

What's your favorite Bible story, Bible verse, or person in the Bible?

These all teach us about life and faith. They help us to live out our faith.

Write your favorite Bible story, verse, or person on your thankful list.

Thankful Session Reflective Questions

Heaven is a very real place. And one day you're going to go there.

If you think heaven is really awesome, add heaven to your thankful list...

Anything else that you think is really awesome, add that, too.

Thankful Session Reflective Questions

Think about your favorite room in your home.

What are some things you're thankful for?

Add those to your thankful list.

Thankful Session Reflective Questions

Some experiences make us happy. Write down experiences that you are thankful for, and yes, you can use any of the suggestions below.

For example:

Swimming on a hot day	Riding a horse
Going to camp	An encouraging word
Helping others	Playing an instrument
Hugs	Giving a gift
Figuring something out	Accomplishing a goal
Being creative	Reading a good book

Thankful Session Reflective Questions

There are things in life that help us…

<u>For example:</u>

- scissors (to cut paper)
- shoestrings (to keep shoes on)
- cups (to hold drinks)
- fingers (to pick up things)

What helpful things are you thankful for?

Add them to your thankful list.

INTRODUCTORY STORY TALK SHEET

Share your

Name:

Hometown:

Family:

School/Work:

Hobbies/Interests/Favorite Foods/Desserts:

End your introduction by answering one of the following questions:

What do you hope to gain from this experience? or

Why are you here today?

Example: What I hope to gain from being here at this retreat is a better understanding of how God is working in my life.

_____

_____

_____

_____

_____

Devotions Worksheet

THINKING IT THROUGH:

When am I doing my devotion?

_____

Who will be listening to my devotion?

_____

Where will I be doing my devotion?

_____

What are some things I've been learning about God or my faith walk?

_____

What are some things that might be important for those in attendance to know about God and their faith?

_____

PRAYING IT THROUGH:

Pray for God to give you a thought or theme for your devotion, keeping in mind the people who are going to be in attendance.

CHOOSING YOUR THEME:

Complete the sentence: I want to encourage others in their faith walk. I want others to know…

_____

i.e. The Holy Spirit is our Helper, Jesus has power over death, God walks with us through difficult times, There is joy in His presence, God wants us to be kind to others, God uses ordinary people to do extraordinary things, God is love, God is forgiving, etc…

Another way to pick a theme is to look in the concordance in your Bible and choose a word, Bible verse, or Bible story that you like.

What's the main point of the Bible verse or story?

_____

_____

NARROWNG IT DOWN:

Now, in one sentence, summarize the main point that you want to make in your devotion. The main point of my devotion is...

_____

_____

You're chosen your theme, now you're ready to add one Story Talk (or more), a verse or bible story, some questions, and don't forget to make your main point. Your opening and closing prayer should reflect your bible point.

LEADING DEVOTIONS:

1. Open with prayer. Short and simple works great!

2. Share a story. Share a personal story that reflects your theme. This story can be a childhood story talk, or lesson you learned story talk, or just something that relates to the theme.

3. Share a Bible verse or Bible story that reflects your theme. If you're sharing a longer Bible story, you may want to summarize the story and read just a few verses of the story.

4. Make your point. This is where you share your devotion theme. You may even use your one sentence summary of your main point to end your devotion.

5. End with prayer. Thank God for who He is, what you've learned, and/or ask God to help you with what you've just talked about during your devotions.